Wit's Treasury

Frontispiece: After William Scrots, *Henry Howard, Earl of Surrey*, 1546.
 (See pp. 65–66).

Wit's Treasury

Renaissance England and the Classics

Stephen Orgel

PENN

UNIVERSITY OF PENNSYLVANIA PRESS

PHILADELPHIA

Published by
University of Pennsylvania Press
Philadelphia, Pennsylvania 19104-4112
www.upenn.edu/pennpress

Printed in the United States of America on acid-free paper
10 9 8 7 6 5 4 3 2 1

Library of Congress Cataloging-in-Publication Data
Names: Orgel, Stephen, author.
Title: Wit's treasury : Renaissance England and the classics / Stephen Orgel.
Description: 1st edition. | Philadelphia : University of Pennsylvania Press, [2021] | Includes bibliographical references and index.
Identifiers: LCCN 2021000701 | ISBN 9780812253276 (hardcover)
Subjects: LCSH: English literature—Early modern, 1500–1700—History and criticism. | English literature—Classical influences. | Classical literature—Appreciation—England. | Classicism—England. | Renaissance—England.
Classification: LCC PR428.C6 O74 2021 | DDC 820.9/003—dc23
LC record available at https://lccn.loc.gov/2021000701

FRONTISPIECE. After William Scrots, *Henry Howard, Earl of Surrey*, 1546. ©National Portrait Gallery, London.

For Leonard Barkan
of course

Contents

List of Illustrations

Acknowledgments

I am indebted to Silvia Bigliazzi for the invitation to present some of the material in Chapters 1 and 3 as the keynote talk at a conference on Sophocles and Shakespeare at the University of Verona, where I found an expert, responsive, and generous audience. That talk appears under the title "How to Be Classical" in *Skenè: Theatre and Drama Studies* 1, no. 2 (Verona, 2019). A part of Chapter 3 was published under the title "English Classical: The Reform of Poetry in Elizabethan England," in *Arion* 27, no. 2 (Fall 2019). James Tatum has been my patient guide through the complexities of both classical prosody and that mysterious title *Palladis Tamia*; Morton Steen Hansen solved a major problem in the frontispiece portrait of the Earl of Surrey; Tom Bishop, James Simpson, Robert Miola, Melissa Zeiger, and Jonathan Crewe provided expert insight at critical moments; Bradin Cormack and Ivan Lupić were my native informants for the Latin Renaissance; Deanne Williams elegantly refashioned the title. I am indebted to two anonymous readers for their enthusiasm and helpful suggestions, and to Jerome Singerman at the Press for his patience, encouragement, and belief in the project. The dedication to Leonard Barkan acknowledges my gratitude for decades of indispensable conversation and deep friendship.

A Note on Quotations

In quotations, u, v, i, j, and w have been normalized, and contractions have been expanded; otherwise, quotations are given as they appear in the editions cited. In the case of early books that do not include page numbers, citations are to signature numbers. Signatures are the marks placed by the printer at the beginning of each gathering, or section, to show how the book is organized. The marks are usually letters or combinations of letters, but they may also be symbols, such as asterisks or pilcrows. Thus sig. A2^{r} means the first side (*recto*) of the second leaf of the gathering marked A. The second side, or *verso*, would be A2^{v}. Shakespeare quotations are from the New Pelican editions, edited by Stephen Orgel and A. R. Braunmuller.

Chapter 1

Classicizing England

My title alludes to Francis Meres's *Palladis Tamia: Wits Treasury; Being the Second Part of Wits Commonwealth*, published in 1598. The book has become famous for its early appreciation of Shakespeare, but its relevance to my project is its assumption that the way to praise contemporary English literature was by comparing it with that of Greece and Rome: through a "Comparative Discourse," Elizabethan England is declared part of *Palladis Tamia*, the treasure house of Pallas Athena. *Tamia* may also include a pun on the name of the river Thames, so an alternative title would be *Athena's Thames*.[1] The parallel with the classics was repeatedly invoked in the period, but it was neither simple nor without ambivalence. Humanism came to England relatively late, and even then much classical scholarship was devoted to biblical exegesis and theology, rather than to the revival of what we think of as the classics. John Colet, Thomas More, and the visiting Erasmus were superb Latinists, but their Latin was a living language, the language of modern literature and philosophy. Nevertheless, Christian humanism emphasized the continuity of ancient wisdom with Christian doctrine, and Erasmus duly compared John Colet to Plato. But though Colet was thoroughly familiar with the modern Platonists Ficino and Pico, he devoted much of his critical energy to interpreting the Epistles of Saint Paul; and Erasmus's Greek for over two decades was put at the service of establishing a correct text of the New Testament, not of reviving ancient philosophy.

Greek was introduced into the English school curriculum after Colet refounded St. Paul's School in 1512. By midcentury it was being regularly taught in the grammar schools, but even by the end of the century, though it was a tremendously prestigious subject, few scholars were sufficiently at home with it to work without a translation at hand. Sir Thomas North's Plutarch was based on the French version of Jacques Amyot, and even the famously scholarly George Chapman used a Latin trot for his Homer. There was unquestionably a good deal of Greek in circulation—rhetorical terms, scientific names, aphorisms; schoolboys studied it, and Cambridge students were required to attend weekly lectures on Greek (Oxford students made fun of them). Nevertheless, the expression "it's all Greek to me" as a trope of incomprehensibility was already proverbial in Shakespeare's day—it appears in *Julius Caesar* (1599), and in Dekker's *Patient Grissel* (1603).

Recent scholarship has shown that England was heavily invested in classical translation, even in Anglo-Saxon times, though there was obviously no settled notion of what a classical style for English would be.[2] But the larger question was always the really elusive one: what would it mean for the principles of humanism to inform literature in the vernacular—how could English literature become "classical," not only classical in imitating the ancients, but classical in the sense subsequently applied to music, classical as opposed to popular, classical as formal, serious, and therefore good.[3] The literary forebears, Chaucer, Gower, Lydgate, continued to be admired, but they lacked "correctness." Nor do the exceptions rescue the English past: Sir Philip Sidney praises Chaucer's *Troilus and Criseyde*, but wonders at his ability to produce it: "I know not whether to mervaile more, either that he in that mistie time could see so clearely, or that wee in this cleare age walke so stumblingly after him."[4] What should English literature look and sound like, what rules should it follow—how can we, in this clear age, not stumble? In short, how can we produce a vernacular literature that is recognizably classical, whether ancient works in translation or modern works on the classical model; make the classics our own; make our own classics? The problem for Sidney is epitomized in Spenser's *Shepheardes Calender*, which is praised, but also criticized because it does things that Theocritus and Virgil did not do. Similarly, English drama for Sidney is defective insofar as it does not emulate Greek and Roman drama. The models, the tradition, are essential.

And originality? This critic was himself surely one of the two most daringly original poets of his age (the other was Marlowe, who was also an excellent classicist), but an adequate defense of poetry required of it stringent constraints on the new, continual deference to the old. There is, however, an element of question-begging in Sidney's *Apologie for Poetrie*: what in the English sixteenth century would constitute being traditional, adhering to tradition? If the tradition is classical, what should classical imply? What elements could stamp a work of vernacular literature or drama or art as classical? What does English classical look like, or sound like? Sidney's own sense of the classical in the *Apologie* appears to us absurdly limited: English plays that do not observe the unities of time and place are said to be not simply incorrect, but incomprehensible; audiences are assumed to be radically unimaginative (so much for *Antony and Cleopatra*). And yet Sidney's critique of English sonnets—that as love poems most are failures because they would not persuade the beloved of the reality of the lover's passion—makes the success of the poetry dependent entirely on its effect on the listener or reader. Though the model is clearly Petrarch, the originals produce no set of rules; and Sidney's own sonnet sequence, while it admirably responds to the critique in the *Apologie*, departs significantly from any Petrarchan model, and explicitly rejects "poor Petrarch's long-deceasèd woes."[5]

But the rejection of a model is also a way of deferring to it. Sidney, rejecting Petrarch, acknowledges the priority of the Italian model, how essential the Italian model is as something to respond to or react against. He substitutes his own woes for Petrarch's; the result, one could say, is a new Petrarchan sonnet sequence—Sidney becomes a new Petrarch. The invocation of Petrarch is an essential part of the narrative. A good deal of energy in the period went into the devising of strategies for becoming the new ancients in this way, strategies of translation and adaptation, and the invention of appropriately classical-sounding models for vernacular verse, the domestication of the classic.

How to Be Classical

The locus classicus, so to speak, was provided by the Earl of Surrey, who in the 1530s translated two books of the *Aeneid* in a style designed to be "classical," a poetic meter intended to serve as an English equivalent to Virgilian hexameters. The meter was what became known as blank verse, and strictly speaking, all that was Virgilian about it was that it was unrhymed. Surrey presumably considered pentameter "natural" to English, as hexameter was to Latin, though in fact the Latin hexameter was not "natural"; it was modeled on the Greek. The assumption was ultimately prophetic, but in the 1530s, it would have seemed very surprising, and the translations, though they must have circulated in manuscript, remained unpublished until well after Surrey's death.

Recent claims for Surrey's influence on Marlowe and Milton are surely unwarranted. When Marlowe translates nondramatic poetry he almost invariably uses couplets (the one exception is his Lucan, discussed below). The blank verse of his drama is for him an innovation, and judging from *Hero and Leander*, if the Virgilian *Dido Queen of Carthage* had been conceived as a little epic, rather than as a play, it would have been in couplets. It has been argued that Surrey is somewhere behind Milton's blank verse, but there was no edition of Surrey's *Aeneid* translation after 1557, and Milton's chief source is surely Shakespeare—*Paradise Lost* was originally conceived as a drama. David Norbrook has argued persuasively that Milton's model for the ten-book 1667 *Paradise Lost* is Lucan's ten-book revolutionary epic *Pharsalia*,[6] but there is no evidence that Milton was aware of Marlowe's blank verse translation of Book 1 of *Pharsalia*, which was published in 1600 and not reissued. Arthur Gorges's and Thomas May's translations of *Pharsalia* (1614, 1629) are in couplets; and in any case Milton, fluent in Latin, would surely not have been working from translations. Milton's application of dramatic blank verse to epic was his own idea, not borrowed from anyone.[7]

As for the blank verse of drama, Robert Cummings suggests that "somebody, possibly Marlowe" first introduced blank verse onto the stage in the 1580s.[8] But Thomas Sackville and Thomas Norton's *Gorboduc* (performed 1561, published 1565) is the first English play in blank verse, followed shortly by George Gascoigne and Francis Kinwelmersh's *Jocasta* (performed 1566, published 1575)—these are playwrights who actually might have been reading Surrey; and there are of course numerous lost plays from the period of which we can say nothing. Marlowe in the prologue to *Tamburlaine* does say he has rescued drama from the verse of "rhyming mother-wits," but what that implies is that he is either unaware of earlier blank-verse drama, or ignoring it; and doubtless the blank verse of *Gorboduc* and *Jocasta*, elite plays composed for court and academic audiences, had little influence on popular theater. Many of the lost plays of Marlowe's era would have been in the rhyming ballad measure of the perennial favorite *Cambises*—the old style remained popular on the popular stage—and Marlowe thinks of himself, not Surrey, as the reformer.

In 1554, seven years after Surrey's execution for treason, the printer John Day issued Surrey's translation of one book of the *Aeneid*, with the following explanation on the title page: "The fourth boke of Virgill, intreating of the love between Aeneas and Dido, translated into English, and drawne into a straunge metre by Henrye, late Earle of Surrey, worthy to be embraced." Blank verse in 1554 is "a strange [that is, foreign] meter," worth domesticating. Historians of prosody explain that the meter was foreign in that it was influenced by the Italian *verso sciolto*—unrhymed hendecasyllables; literally "free (or open) verse"—which by the sixteenth century was being used as an Italian equivalent to classical hexameters. But how strange it also was is clear from the bafflement registered by such contemporary critics as Roger Ascham, Gabriel Harvey, and William Webbe as late as the 1590s. Webbe says that Surrey "translated . . . some part of Virgil into verse indeed, but without regard of true quantity of syllables."[9] Such critics assumed Surrey was attempting to write quantitatively (that is, with the meter determined not by stress, but by the length of syllables, as is the case in Greek and Latin poetry), or that he should have been doing so, and therefore, naturally, found all sorts of mistakes. For such readers, the only verse that sounded classical was quantitative verse, which did seem to have a real future in the English 1590s; Sidney in the *Apologie* argues for both the ancient and the modern systems, "there beeing in eyther sweetnes, and wanting in neither majesty," and intersperses a number of exemplary quantitative lyrics among the accentual poems included in the *Arcadia*. He also asserts, in a wonderful bit of linguistic imperialism, that "Truely the English, before any other vulgar language I know, is fit for both sorts"—he considers it superior to Latin as a language for poetry, and outclassed only by Greek.[10]

To those for whom quantitative verse alone was properly poetic, blank verse would certainly be "strange," but in fact, there was nothing foreign about it. Surrey may have been imitating *versi sciolti*, but he was writing in Chaucer's meter, simply without the rhyme. Possibly it was not recognized as Chaucer's meter because by the sixteenth century the culture had forgotten how to read Chaucer; Chaucer was perfectly regular in middle English, but sounded rough as pronunciation changed, and especially as the final *e*'s were no longer sounded.

In 1557, three years after John Day's edition of Surrey's *Aeneid* IV, Richard Tottel issued, in the space of less than two months, what was essentially Surrey's complete works: both the second and fourth books of the *Aeneid* in blank verse, and two separate editions of *Songes and Sonettes Written By the Ryght Honorable Lord Henry Howard, late Earle of Surrey, and other*—the volume that has become known as Tottel's Miscellany. The principal "other" was Thomas Wyatt. Wyatt and Surrey were all at once major poets, but Surrey was the benchmark. Wyatt's irregular metrics were therefore duly revised to accord with Surrey's style. Tottel, that is, understood that Surrey's verse was "regular," and was not a bungled attempt at quantitative metrics.

Tottel clearly expected some resistance. In a brief and acerbic preface, he writes, "If perhappes some mislike the statelyness of style removed from the rude skil of common eares: I aske helpe of the learned to defende theyr learned frendes, the authors of this woorke: And I exhort the unlearned, by reading to learne to be more skilful, and to purge that swinelike grossenesse that maketh the sweete majerome [marjoram] not to smel to their delight."[11] Pigs were said to hate the smell of marjoram—unsophisticated readers are pigs. Surrey's "stateliness of style" is something unfamiliar, but also educated and aristocratic. It is what English poetry should aspire to; as John Day had said, it is "worthy to be embraced." In contrast, Tottel's edition of the *Aeneid* translation makes no special claims. The title page says only "Certain Bokes of Virgiles Aeneis turned into English meter"—Tottel, unlike Day, markets blank verse not as "strange," but as English. And unlike the *Songes and Sonnettes*, Tottel's *Aeneid* edition has no apology or justification, no critical harangue, not even the usual dedicatory and commendatory verses. The poem begins at once, on the next leaf: this is, quite simply, English Virgil.

But English classicists, even those who were not attempting quantitative verse, were without exception unconvinced. Surrey's blank verse seems, in the history of English prosody, revolutionary, but it did not start a revolution; and blank verse was reinvented several times before it became a norm. What was really new about Surrey's Virgil, as James Simpson has brilliantly argued, was the elimination of the translator's voice, the abolition of fifteen hundred years of reading and commentary. The only voice in this work in sixteenth-century English purports to be that of Virgil.[12]

In 1558, the year after Tottel published Surrey's Virgil, the first seven books of Thomas Phaer's *Aeneid* appeared. Phaer's English classical verse was fourteener couplets (the translation was eventually completed by Thomas Twine in 1584). In 1565 Arthur Golding's first four books of Ovid's *Metamorphoses* "Translated Oute of Latin into Englishe Meter" were published. Golding's English meter was again rhyming fourteeners. The complete translation appeared in 1567, and was continuously in print for half a century; the Elizabethan classical meter was essentially a ballad measure. By 1595 the verse could already be parodied by Shakespeare in *A Midsummer Night's Dream*, when Bottom suddenly breaks into a bit of old-fashioned classicism:

> The raging rocks
> And shivering shocks
> Shall break the locks
> Of prison gates;
> And Phibbus' car
> Shall shine from far,
> And make and mar
> The foolish fates. (1.2.27–34)

In 1621 Golding's Ovidian fourteeners were finally superseded not by blank verse, but by pentameter couplets, with the publication of the first five books of George Sandys's translation of the *Metamorphoses*, completed in 1626. This set the standard for English Ovid for the next two centuries. Sandys is Ovid in a style that looks to us recognizably neoclassical.

As for the *Aeneid* after Phaer, Richard Stanyhurst's version of the first four books in "English heroical verse" was first published in Leiden in 1582. English heroical verse in this case was quantitative hexameters—genuinely classical, though finally not English enough. A second edition was published in London in the next year, but there was no subsequent edition until antiquarians rediscovered it in the nineteenth century. Nevertheless, Stanyhurst's *Aeneid* marks a significant moment of transition, and we shall return to it.

The English Virgilian tradition may be said to have developed a norm when Ben Jonson, near the end of his play *Poetaster* (performed 1601), has Virgil recite a passage from the *Aeneid*, and his prosody was pentameter couplets. Although Phaer and Twine's *Aeneid* continued to be the standard translation (the last edition was in 1612), the pentameter couplet had become "classic."

Refiguring the Classics

The refiguring of the classics into English was not a novelty, and it did not begin with Surrey. The enduring prestige of translation in England may be gauged by Chaucer's claim that his *Troilus and Criseyde* is not original, but derives from the work of an otherwise unknown Roman poet named Lollius. The fictitious classical author provides a degree of authority missing from Chaucer's real source, Boccaccio's *Filostrato*—contemporary, not ancient; Italian, not Latin. A more puzzling example may indicate the prestige of specifically English translation: Marie de France claimed to have translated her Aesop not from the Greek, but from a version in Old English by Alfred the Great, a royal source. No trace of this work, nor any other reference to it, survives.

But pervasive as the knowledge of the classics surely was in medieval England, translation was neither systematic nor comprehensive. To begin with, as Stephen Medcalf points out, "As long as to be literate normally involved belonging to the clergy, whose language was Latin, the Latin classics were a literary heritage to be retold, continued or imitated, like the *Aeneid* in Geoffrey of Monmouth's *Historia Regum Britanniae*, but there was no great point in translating them."[13] Here, in addition to the examples already discussed, are the highlights up to 1600, including a few surprises. The principal surviving Anglo-Saxon example is a Boethius from the ninth or tenth century. There are in addition saints' lives, and an adaptation of Lactantius. But there is also a fragment of an eleventh-century Old English translation of the Greek romance *Apollonius of Tyre*, which suggests that there was a good deal more of which we have no record (and there certainly may have been an Aesop).[14]

According to Rita Copeland, the most widely adapted ancient authors in medieval England were (in addition to Boethius, Virgil, and some Ovid) Statius and Lucan.[15] These two poets may provide a good index to how much of a transformation humanism effected on the canon: the first printed English edition of Lucan was not published until 1589 (which means, probably after Marlowe did his translation), the second in 1618; and the first English edition of Statius did not appear until 1651. Nevertheless, Stuart Gillespie observes that Statius's influence throughout the English Renaissance was pervasive, and "as late a figure as Pope considers Statius 'of the old Latin poets . . . next in merit to those of the Augustan age.'"[16] Statius and Lucan, then, were being read in editions published on the continent; but it must be to the point that English publishers did not anticipate a sufficient market for domestic editions. As for translations, after Marlowe's version of the first book of Lucan, published in 1600 (composed at least a decade earlier), there were Arthur Gorges's translation in 1618, and, starting in 1629, multiple editions of Thomas May's translation, along with his continuation of the epic up to the death of Julius Caesar, issued throughout the century. By the 1630s there was a healthy audience for the revolutionary epic. But Statius's *Thebaid* was not translated until 1648, by an otherwise unknown schoolmaster named Thomas Stephens; and there was no second edition.

Boethius is the only classical author Chaucer translated (if we except the chimerical Lollius), though Chaucer was obviously thoroughly familiar with Ovid, Virgil, and the corpus of Trojan War stories; and his skill at translation was in his own time a point of praise. Eustache Deschamps, in his *Ballade* on Chaucer, celebrates him specifically as a "grant translateur,"[17] referring presumably to his version of the *Roman de la Rose,* and perhaps also the *Filostrato.* The only English Cicero before the sixteenth century was the translations of *De Senectute* and *De Amicitia* from French versions, issued by Caxton, and the only Ovid was Caxton's *Metamorphoses,* a prose translation also based on a French prose version, which survives in a single manuscript and was never published—oddly: could Caxton not have considered it marketable? Caxton published a prose *Aeneid, Eneydos* (1490), which also derives from a French version. Nevertheless, by the 1490s Henry VII's poet laureate, the humanist cleric Bernard André, was writing his celebratory *Historia Henrici Septimi* not in English but in Latin. An allegorization of Henry's triumph modeled on the Labors of Hercules is also attributed to André—the latter, despite the classical context, was in French (it was clearly intended for courtly readers). The first Tudor monarch, invader and usurper, insisted on his right to the throne through his impeccably British credentials, but his poet laureate wrote exclusively in Latin or French. Neither work was printed; both survive only in presentation manuscripts—André's audience was small, exclusive, aristocratic, and learned. David Carlson writes that what is "distinctive about André's Latin verse, both political and religious, is his willingness to try ancient lyric metres at a time when these were little practiced in England, and the pervasive classicism of his verse, apparent even in his religious poetry."[18] Similarly, the first English secular drama, Henry Medwall's *Fulgens and Lucres* (ca. 1497), which centers on a debate about the relative claims of noble birth versus inner merit that is clearly a celebration of Henry's new meritocratic aristocracy, is nevertheless set in ancient Rome (discussed in Chapter 6). Humanism had arrived, and at the highest level of society.

In the next century Thomas Drant published a translation of Horace's *Ars Poetica* and two books of the *Satires* in 1566 and 1567, both in fourteener couplets—up to that point there had been only two Horace poems in print in English. The ten tragedies ascribed to Seneca were translated between 1559 and 1581; nine of these, like the Horace, were in fourteener couplets (one, *Octavia*, was in pentameter couplets; none was in blank verse). A partial translation of Caesar's *Gallic War* based on a French version had appeared in 1530; Arthur Golding did a complete translation from the Latin in 1565. The first bits of Tacitus did not appear until 1591. As we have seen, Marlowe's translation of the first book of Lucan's *Pharsalia* appeared in 1600, seven years after his death and the year after his Ovid *Amores*. The Lucan alone of all the English classics was in blank verse, and was the only volume of Marlowe's verse that was never reissued. It presumably dates from the mid-1580s, his college years, and for publishers by 1600 it would have constituted the bottom of the Marlowe barrel.

Often translation was, logically, in the service of teaching Latin. Abraham Fleming's version of Virgil's *Eclogues* and *Georgics* was published in 1575 and again in 1589, as he says in a preface, "for the profit and furtherance of English youths desirous to learne, and delighted in poetrie . . . , not in foolish rime . . . but in due proportion and measure . . . that yoong Grammar boyes, may even without a schoolemaister teach themselves by the help thereof."[19] Fleming's "due proportion and measure" is not, as one might expect, quantitative verse, but unrhymed fourteeners. The translation is quite literal, and scrupulously places in brackets words that have been included either to satisfy the demands of English grammar or to fill out the meter. And although Terence was part of the academic curriculum both in the classroom and in performance, the only translation of the plays was Nicholas Udall's *Floures for Latine spekynge selected and gathered oute of Terence, and the same translated in to Englysshe, together with the exposition and settynge forthe as welle of suche latyne wordes, as were thought nedefull to be annoted, as also of dyvers grammatical rules, very profytable [and] necessarye for the expedite knowledge in the latine tongue*, published in 1534, and in subsequent editions throughout the century. The Flowers are taken from three plays, *Andria*, *Eunuchus*, and *Heautontimoroumenos*; and as the title indicates, the volume offers only renderings of exemplary bits of dialogue. Terence was here presented as a model not for comedy, but for Latin conversation.

Figure 1 is one of the surprises. In 1588, William Byrd published a setting of a bit of Ovid's *Heroides*, the opening eight lines of Penelope's epistle to Ulysses, translated by an anonymous poet into English quantitative measures. This example is unique in Byrd's vast oeuvre: even when Byrd set Latin quantitative poems, he did not set them quantitatively. But Byrd understood the scansion perfectly, setting long syllables to half notes and short syllables to quarter notes. The music even corrects three errors in the metrics (these are outlined in the reproduction). Byrd's amendment of the scansion is a tiny indication of how actively involved in the issue of poetic quantity English culture actually was at this time. The poem is always ascribed to Thomas Watson, because he was acquainted with Byrd and wrote at least one (nonquantitative) song text for him. But I doubt that this can be right: Watson was a thoroughly proficient classicist, who wrote much more Latin poetry than English. He would not have made mistakes in composing hexameters. Byrd was more expert than his poet here.[20]

Another surprise: a single epigram of Martial's, the poem to himself on the good life ("*Vitam quae faciunt beatiorem*"), translated by the Welsh poet Simon Vachan into both Welsh couplets and English rhyme royal, appeared in 1571 on a broadsheet, presumably to be sold as ballads were (a translation into quatrains had earlier been done by Surrey, and appears in

Figure 1. Constant Penelope, from William Byrd, *Psalmes, Sonets, & songs of sadnes and pietie*, 1588. The musical corrections of the scansion are outlined.

Tottel, *Songes and Sonnettes*; and Sir Thomas Elyot translated four lines from the poem, along with some other classical fragments, in *The Governour*). The first English Horace, two satires full of dire examples of misspent lives translated into fourteener couplets in 1565 by Lewis Evans, schoolmaster (judging from the name, another Welshman), had similarly been printed to be sold as single sheets.[21] Though substantial translations of Horace appeared soon afterward, the next Martial in English was not published till 1629.

There was no Catullus until Jonson's Volpone attempted to seduce Celia with a translation of "Vivamus mea Lesbia" in 1606; no Lucretius until the 1650s, no Tibullus until 1694, and not even a Latin text of Propertius until 1697. The first British *Aeneid*, translated by Gavin Douglas into Scots dialect in 1513 (not published till 1553) had been in loose pentameter couplets, a striking premonition; but as anomalous for the English tradition for most of the century as it was for the Scots. Indeed, the translation was, in a sense, well in advance of its time, and Douglas prefaced it with an elaborate apology to Virgil:

> Quhy suld I than, with dull forhede and vane
> With rude ingyne, and barane emptiue brane
> With bad harsk spech, and lewit barbare toung
> Presume to write, quhare thy sueit bell is roung

The answer is simply so "that thy fecund sentence, mycht be soung / In our langage, als weil as latyne toung,"[22] an acknowledgment of the growing importance of vernacular literacy.

The Greek classics, not surprisingly, got a later start, though a number of works were published in Greek in England, and by the midcentury it was a prestigious subject of study—the schoolboy notebooks of King Edward VI, who died at the age of fifteen, include fifty essays in Greek, along with fifty-five in Latin. The STC records thirty-two titles printed during Elizabeth's reign that are wholly or largely in Greek—that is a minuscule number compared with the number of Latin books produced in the period, but it does indicate that there were available typesetters and proofreaders, and a real if limited market. The Greek titles appeared for the most part in the 1580s and 1590s, and are not only schoolbooks and religious texts; in 1553 the printer Reyner Wolfe had issued

George Etheridge's translation of the second book of Virgil's *Aeneid* into Greek. Printers in London, Oxford, and Cambridge produced texts by Homer, Aristophanes, Demosthenes, and Plutarch. As Kirsty Milne writes, "It is of course possible that some were printed as one-off ventures, experiments to test the market or boutique orders from a patron. But their survival indicates, at least, that English printers had the equipment and the expertise to produce Greek books, and thought it worth their while to do so. At most, it suggests a need to reappraise the role of Greek in late sixteenth-century intellectual and cultural life."[23] She points out that since the London printer John Day produced a Greek *Trojan Women* in 1575, George Gascoigne and Francis Kinwelmersh's *Jocasta*, itself adapted from an Italian version (performed in 1566, published in 1575), did not constitute England's only access to Euripides.[24]

As for translations of the major prose works, the first Thucydides in English appeared in 1550, Herodotus in 1584. The first comprehensive Aristotle was a translation of the *Politics* from the French published in 1598; Leonardo Bruni's Latin translation of the *Ethics* had been published by a short-lived Oxford press in 1479,[25] and an English summary of the *Ethics* appeared in 1547. A Latin translation of the *Poetics* was published in 1623 and the Greek text in 1696, but no English version appeared until 1705, and that, like the *Politics* over a century earlier, was based on a French translation. (Most of the English works ascribed to Aristotle in the period consisted of versions of "Aristotle's Masterpiece" or "Secrets of Aristotle," spurious gynecological and medical handbooks—*Aristotle's Masterpiece* went on being published into the twentieth century.) Though Plato is frequently cited, there were no English editions of any of the dialogues, and the only sixteenth-century English translation was of the Hellenistic *Axiochus*, published in 1592 (when it was thought to be by Plato) and credited to one "Edward Spenser." The name is apparently merely an inexpert marketing strategy: there is no evidence connecting the poet with this work.[26] The first authentic Platonic dialogues to appear in English translations were the *Apology* and the *Phaedo*, published anonymously in 1675.[27]

Milnes's cautionary observation about "one-off ventures, experiments to test the market or boutique orders from a patron" needs to be kept in mind—the Greek translation of *Aeneid* II is surely an example; so is the 1479 Oxford *Ethics*.[28] Most of the Greek works, whether in the original language or in translation, were published only once—the market in England was obviously not large. The only sixteenth-century prose translation from the Greek popular enough to appear in multiple editions was the romance novel *Aethiopica* of Heliodorus, first published in 1569 and reissued six times by 1627. The Thucydides was based on a French version, the Heliodorus on a Latin one. Only the Herodotus appears to derive directly from the Greek.[29]

Of verse, the first Theocritus translation, published anonymously in 1588, is, like most of the Latin translations, in hexameter and fourteener couplets, with the last of the idylls in trimeter couplets. The only attempt at dramatic translation, aside from the Euripidean *Jocasta* (of which more presently), was Jane, Lady Lumley's *Iphigenia in Aulis*, in the 1550s, in prose, and unpublished; and George Peele's translation of one of the *Iphigenia* plays, performed by Paul's Boys sometime in the 1570s, also unpublished, and now lost. Queen Elizabeth studied Greek with Roger Ascham and was said to have translated a play of Euripides, of which nothing more is known. Thomas Watson's Latin *Antigone* appeared in 1581; the play had apparently been performed—Gabriel Harvey saw it in London, or perhaps in Cambridge. The manuscript of an English version of *Oedipus* for performance by schoolboys, prepared around the turn of the century, was recently acquired by the Elizabethan Club at Yale. It is in fourteener couplets, and includes comic scenes and two songs, one with the music. It has nothing to do with Sophocles: it gives the whole story, including the abandonment of the infant Oedipus (one of the songs is a lullaby) and the encounter with the sphinx; and much of it is, verbatim, Alexander Neville's midcentury translation of the *Oedipus* of Seneca.[30] It certainly does not imply that either the masters who prepared the text or the schoolboys who performed it had any familiarity with the Greek play.

The only attempt at a Homer before Chapman was Arthur Hall's 1581 translation of ten books of the *Iliad* into fourteener couplets, based on a French verse translation. Chapman's *Iliad*, published beginning in 1598, is also in the by-now-antiquated (or "classic") fourteener couplets, though the account of Achilles's shield from Book 18, published separately in the same year, is in pentameter couplets. For the final version of the complete poem, published in 1611, Achilles's shield was redone in fourteeners, to accord with the rest. By 1616, for the *Odyssey*, Chapman had switched to pentameter couplets.

The standard had again been set by Marlowe, with his thrilling adaptation of Musaeus's *Hero and Leander*, pentameter couplets like his Ovid—by the turn of the century this was the voice of English classicism; though it has to be added that Marlowe's little epic is not very much like Musaeus's, even with Chapman's dutiful continuation. Nevertheless Chapman, returning to the poem in 1616 to produce a proper translation (the title page declares it "Translated according to the original"), casts it in pentameter couplets.

In short, the poets interested in Surrey's blank verse were mainly the dramatists, starting in the 1560s, but (judging from what survives) not regularly till late in the century—the midcentury academic plays based on Plautus and Terence, *Gammer Gurton's Needle*, *Ralph Roister Doister*, *Jack Juggler*, are all in loose hexameter couplets. Subsequently, with a very few exceptions such as Gascoigne's Ovidian satire *The Steele Glas* and Marlowe's translation of Lucan, blank verse was useful not as a rendering of classical verse but for dramatic dialogue.[31] As a version of classical verse it served for Seneca in *Gorboduc* (the first English play in blank verse), though not, as we have seen, for translations of Seneca; for Euripides in *Jocasta*, Gascoigne and Francis Kinwelmersh's version of *The Phoenician Women*, though not for Lady Lumley's *Iphigenia*; for Plautus in *The Comedy of Errors*, Terence in *The Taming of the Shrew* (in both cases liberally interspersed with couplets, and in *Errors* at one point with old-fashioned rhyming hexameters); and for English drama of the period generally, for Kyd, Marlowe, Shakespeare, Jonson, producing an English classic theater. But after Surrey, with the single exception of Gascoigne, never for English Virgil, Ovid, Homer. Those required another kind of "classical."

English epics, moreover, significantly, were nothing like any of these: the stanzaic verse of Spenser, Drayton, Daniel derived from the Chaucer of *Troilus*, from rhyme royal, from Ariosto, Boiardo, Tasso—Sir John Harington's translation of *Orlando Furioso* (1591) showed how successfully the Italian style could be domesticated. The classic models here were those of the romance tradition; and even they had started to sound unnatural by the late seventeenth century. In 1687 an anonymous "Person of Quality" brought *The Faerie Queene* up to date, as the title page advertised, with Spenser's "Essential Design preserv'd, but his obsolete Language and manner of Verse totally laid aside. Deliver'd in Heroick Numbers."[32] The heroic numbers were, by now inevitably, pentameter couplets.

Milton, a century after Surrey, was still bucking the tide in declaring blank verse to be the natural language of English epic poetry. Thanks to Marlowe, the pentameter couplet had, almost overnight, become the classical standard.

For English poetry, the 1580s were a decade of profound stylistic ambivalence. George Gascoigne had been an adventurous poet, and in hindsight appears to be a transitional figure; indeed, a volume of collected poems was issued in 1587, ten years after his death. He had wide interests and wrote in a number of poetic formats—prose and verse drama, hexameter couplets, rhyme royal, pentameter quatrains, poulter's measure, even blank verse in *The Steele Glas*—though he had never used the verse of the future, pentameter couplets (surprisingly, because it was also the verse of the past: he acknowledged Chaucer as his model). But by 1587 taste had moved on; Gascoigne was already outdated, and there was no subsequent edition of the poems. The volume turned out to be a monument, not a harbinger. The crucial transitional figures from our point of view are Marlowe, the Ovidian outsider, both notorious and admired for violating all the norms, poetic and social, but thereby creating a new norm for poetry, and the Virgilian Spenser, working within the system but no less revolutionary.

Chapter 2

The Uses of Prosody

Ovidian Marlowe

Christopher Marlowe was the son of a Canterbury shoemaker, christened two months before Shakespeare, in February 1564. We know nothing of his childhood, but at the age of fourteen he was granted a scholarship to the King's School in Canterbury. His education there would have been heavily classical, and he clearly emerged as an excellent classicist; but since his tenure at the school was little over a year, he must already have been very proficient when he entered. In 1581 he obtained a scholarship to Corpus Christi College, Cambridge, where he remained for seven years, earning a BA in 1584 and an MA in 1587. During this time he was apparently employed as an agent of the Privy Council, a government spy providing intelligence about recusants and expatriate Roman Catholics. The conferral of his Cambridge degree was delayed because of suspicions about his loyalty and was only awarded after an assurance was provided by the council that he had done good service to the crown.

After his college years, we know little about his life until the end of it. He was killed in a tavern brawl—or more likely assassinated in what was represented as a tavern brawl—in 1593, when he was not yet thirty years old. In those six years, whatever else he was doing, he revolutionized English drama and gave a new voice to Elizabethan poetry.[1] Most of what we must use to construct a biography is either speculation from contextual information, or gossip and invective, largely posthumous. In 1588 *Tamburlaine* was accused by Robert Greene of promoting atheism, yet *Tamburlaine* was not ascribed to Marlowe until the nineteenth century, and there is no reason to assume that a reference to the drama, or its hero, is a reference to Marlowe. However, the circle of Elizabethan writers was small, and Greene may have known that Marlowe wrote the play; Gabriel Harvey may have known it too.[2] In any case, the charge of atheism kept recurring. After Marlowe's death, Thomas Kyd, who had shared lodgings with him, testified to his "vile heretical conceits denying the divinity of Jesus." William Baines, a paid informer, provided more lurid testimony about Marlowe's dangerous opinions. Among these, according to Baines, were that Moses was a juggler—a mountebank, a charlatan—and that Thomas Harriot, Sir Walter Ralegh's servant, "can do more than he." This has always been taken as an invidious comparison of Harriot with Moses, but it may include something in its way equally subversive, a claim that Ralegh's servant was better than his master. Marlowe also believed, Baines said, that "the first beginning of religion was only to keep men in awe"; that Jesus was a bastard, his mother a whore, his father a carpenter, and the crucifixion fully justified; that Roman Catholicism was a good religion and "all Protestants are hypocritical asses"; that the woman of Samaria and her sister were whores and Jesus knew them "dishonestly"; that Jesus was the "bedfellow" of John the Evangelist and "used him as the sinners of Sodom"; that all those who loved not tobacco and boys were fools; and that he had as much right to issue currency as the queen of England.[3] This looks like a jumble, and is certainly rife with contradictions; but in its cultural context the charges have a basic consistency, assuming a world in which heresy, scurrility, sodomy, counterfeiting, social mobility, and the drive toward success are all aspects of the same dangerous set of desires.[4]

Since Baines was being paid to provide damaging testimony, it would have been in his interest to make Marlowe out to be as disreputable as possible. Still, there is much in the poetry and drama to support the picture of Marlowe as a subversive, seductively persuasive radical, exemplifying both the power and the danger of a classical education—he brought into English not only the erotic Ovid and Musaeus, but the revolutionary Lucan; and he was, after all, a government spy (and if his murder was an assassination, even the spymasters distrusted him). Did this result in the proscription of his work? Not, certainly, of his drama: both during his lifetime and long after, his plays were among the most popular in the repertory. As for the poems, *Hero and Leander,* published in 1598, immediately became a classic. The Ovid translations, published in 1599, were called in, banned and burned by episcopal order; but it is not clear in this case that the proscription was aimed at Marlowe. The banned book was a collection of satirical epigrams by John Davies followed by ten of Marlowe's translations from the *Amores*—"Davyes Epigrams, with Marlowes Elegys" is the way the order puts it. The offensive material may well have been Davies's, and the offense thus libel, not incitement to lechery. As the book is constituted, Marlowe is at most guilty by association: all six early editions of the Ovid translations include Davies's epigrams, though those with the complete elegies put Marlowe first, and all are published either abroad, at Middleburgh, in Holland, or surreptitiously in Scotland with a false Middleburgh imprint. If Davies was the problem, why not publish Marlowe's Ovid by itself? Or was it the scurrilous Davies that sold the erotic Marlowe? Would a Marlowe untainted by libel not have been marketable?

Marlowe's translation of the *Amores, All Ovids Elegies*, was unpublished during Marlowe's lifetime. After his death, the manuscript would have recommended itself to publishers not merely as the work of Marlowe the erotic classicist, cashing in on the success of *Hero and Leander*, but equally as the first translation of the *Amores* not only into English but into any modern language. The *Amores* was the least well known of Ovid's works to the Renaissance, untouched by the allegorizing and moralizing commentaries that had safely contextualized Ovid's other work for Christian readers. Marlowe's interest in these poems would have been as much in their urbanity of tone as in their world of erotic possibilities—the social Ovid is fully complementary to the mythological Ovid of the *Metamorphoses* and the *Fasti*. But Marlowe's Ovidian elegies are more than translations. They undertake, with remarkable energy and ingenuity, the adaptation of a quintessentially classical mode to the uses of English poetry. In a sense, this is Marlowe's sonnet sequence, the psychic drama of a poet-lover whose love is both his creation and his ultimate monomania, frustration, despair. The excitement Marlowe brought to these poems is obvious, as much in the vividness and wit of the language as in the evident haste and occasional carelessness of the composition. The six early editions, and the heavy hand of the ecclesiastical censor, testify to the excitement readers got out of the work. But licentiousness is not the *Elegies*' primary claim on our attention; indeed, by current standards they are barely warm. Their rhetoric, however, brings a new tone and a new range of possibilities into English verse. Donne's elegies are full of a sense of Marlowe's language, which looks forward, too, to Carew and Marvell, and even to Pope.

Nevertheless, *All Ovids Elegies* is a strange book. It reads like a promising first draft, occasionally felicitous but often routine, with moments of real brilliance but also moments of striking ineptitude, and even errors—these are often the errors of the edition he is using, but not invariably. Time after time the only way to understand Marlowe's English is to use the Latin as a crib. "So, chaste Minerva, did Cassandra fall / Deflowered except, within thy temple wall" (1.7)—the Latin says that the only chastity left to Cassandra was the fact that she was raped in Minerva's temple; it is difficult to see how one would get this out of the English. "Hector to arms went from his wife's embraces, / And on Andromache his helmet laces" (1.9)—only the Latin will reveal that it is Andromache who is lacing the helmet on Hector, not the other way round. "Object thou then what she may well excuse, / To stain in faith all truth, by all crimes use" (2.2)—the Latin says "accuse her only of what she can explain away; a false charge undermines the credibility of a true one": is there any way of eliciting this from Marlowe? "Wilt thou her fault learn, she may make thee tremble; / Fear to be guilty, then thou mayst dissemble" (2.2)—even the Latin will not help to explain this. Often the gibberish is undeniably beautiful, the work of a poet with a superb ear working too fast for meaning: "What day was that which, all sad haps to bring / White birds to lovers did not always sing" (3.11)—Ovid says, this is the day when, as a permanent bad omen, lovebirds stopped singing; but Marlowe's version is all connotation with no denotation.

Even so, the translation is an impressive achievement, especially if, as appears to be the case, it is the work of Marlowe's undergraduate years; and its completeness is not the least of its virtues. It remained unique in English until an anonymous translation appeared in 1683, followed by Dryden. As for its occasional impenetrability, the Elizabethans had a higher tolerance for obscurity than we have. What Marlowe undertook was the domestication of the erotic Ovid in the wake of the many previous generations' mythographic

Ovid. And after Marlowe's sensational death, the combination of Ovid, Marlowe, and English would probably have been sufficient to warrant publication surreptitiously, even if John Davies's scurrilous epigrams had not been included. But since the erotic Marlowe looms so large in the modern construction of the poet, it is worth pausing over the sexuality of *All Ovids Elegies*. How erotically transgressive is it?

Transgressive enough, certainly: it is a chronicle not merely of lechery, but of adultery, pandering, promiscuity, faithlessness, irreverence. It is even, on occasion, explicit and smutty where Ovid is merely metonymic: "The whore stands to be bought for each man's money, / And seeks vile wealth by selling of her coney" (1.10.21–22), where the Latin specifies only "*corpore*," her body.[5] Ovid's urbane cynicism in English, moreover, translates directly into Marlowe's alleged atheism: "God is a name, no substance, feared in vain, / And doth the world in fond belief detain" (3.3.23–24). Reason enough to publish the book surreptitiously. Still, it is the nature of the eroticism we should pause over. Since Marlowe's homosexual interests figure so significantly in both Baines's and Kyd's charges against him, and are certainly manifest in *Edward II*, the opening of *Dido Queen of Carthage*, and *Hero and Leander*, and are especially prominent in the construction of the modern Marlowe, it is worth observing that the erotics of *All Ovid's Elegies* are exclusively heterosexual—not even Cupid in elegy 1.10 (15–17), a beautiful naked youth selling himself, without so much as a pocket to put his money in, raises Marlowe's rhetorical eyebrow. Ovid himself observes that his sexual interests are primarily in women: he says in the *Ars Amatoria* that the sex he likes is the kind that gives equal pleasure to both partners, and he is therefore not much interested in sex with boys (2.683–84)—the "therefore" made sense to Roman readers because the boy, as the passive partner in the buggery, was supposed not to enjoy the sex, a prophylactic fiction designed to license the practice of pederasty while simultaneously preserving the youth of the realm from any suspicion of real depravity.[6] If Marlowe's erotic imagination was essentially homosexual, and sex was the point, Catullus, Martial, Horace, or even the Virgil of the *Eclogues* would surely have been more likely texts for domestication. Was it then something other than the sex that attracted him to the *Amores*?

Perhaps so: a case can be made for the young Marlowe's translation of the *Amores* as part of a grand design, the first step in the creation of a poetic career consciously modeled on Ovid, an anti-Virgilian, and anti-Spenserian, model.[7] This may be correct; nevertheless, the sex may well have been a factor after all: perhaps the whole question is anachronistic, the issue construed too narrowly. Perhaps, in short, homosexuality is our problem, not Marlowe's. The first published account of his murder, Thomas Beard's in *The Theatre of Gods Judgements*, 1597, specifies epicurism and atheism as Marlowe's mortal sins.[8] In the next year, Francis Meres cites Beard, and adds the information, derived from no known source, that Marlowe "was stabd to death by a bawdy Serving-man, a rivall of his in his lewde love"[9]—is this perhaps merely an expansion of the implications of epicurism? Charles Nicholl has elaborated the account still further by suggesting that "this serving-man was, like Marlowe, a homosexual, and that the cause of the fight, the object of their 'lewd love,' was another man."[10] Marlowe's sexual preferences are not really in question, but this surely confuses the issue. To begin with, there is no reason to assume that Meres has a love triangle in mind; "rival" can mean simply "partner" (as Bernardo calls Horatio and Marcellus "the rivals of my watch" at the opening of *Hamlet*), and if we want Marlowe's "lewd love" to be homosexual, its object may simply be the bawdy serving man. But it is surely to the point that the object is unspecified, the crime "epicurism," the pursuit of pleasure. The sin is precisely the subject of the *Amores*, "lewd love," illicit sexuality, of whatever kind—if homosexuality had been a worse kind of "lewd love," Marlowe would have been guilty of it. A century later Antony à Wood elaborated Meres's account for his age as revealingly as Nicholl has done for ours: "For so it fell out that he being deeply in love with a certain woman . . . had for his rival a bawdy serving-man, one rather fit to be a pimp than an ingenious amoretto as Marlowe conceived himself to be."[11]

In fact, homosexuality in the charges against Marlowe is primarily an aspect of his blasphemy and atheism—Baines and Kyd do not assert that Marlowe was a sodomite, but that he said Jesus and St. John were: this is apparently worse than being a sodomite oneself. As for "all they that love not tobacco and boys be fools," the link between the love of boys and the love of tobacco is an intriguing one, but it is not part of a claim that Marlowe systematically debauched the youth of London, as it might well have been. Though his own works could easily have been used as evidence against him, the charge of sodomy appears almost marginal. Commentators have undertaken to connect tobacco to the charge of atheism, noting its source in the pagan New World, but this seems to me misguided. The point is the same one Jonson makes when, in *Every Man Out of his Humour*, the rustic would-be gentleman Sogliardo is discovered at a London tavern with "his villainous Ganymede . . . droning a tobacco pipe there ever since yesterday noon" (4.3.83–85). Sogliardo here is certainly assumed to be guilty of the abominable crime against nature, but this is not the issue. Sodomy and smoking are generic vices, not specific ones: Sogliardo practices them because they are the marks of the London sophisticate. His lust is, like Marlowe's, all for upward mobility, for class. The more intriguing conjunction in Baines's document is that of tobacco and Thomas Harriot. It leads us to Sir Walter Ralegh, Harriot's patron and employer, the major advocate of tobacco in Elizabethan England, investigated in 1594 on a charge of freethinking; imprisoned, however, not for atheism but for impregnating and secretly marrying, probably in that order, one of Elizabeth's maids of honor—for sexual offenses that were construed as presumptuous enough to be treasonable. Thomas Kyd's charges against Marlowe explicitly associate him with the Ralegh circle, which included not only Harriot, but John Dee and Henry Percy, the "Wizard Earl" of Northumberland (of whom the *DNB* says he was "passionately addicted to tobacco smoking"). With Ralegh we are back to atheism and sex, but with Harriot, Dee, and Northumberland we have arrived at conjuring and science, the world of Marlowe's most famous play, *Doctor Faustus*.

Marlowe's greatest achievement as poet and classicist is certainly *Hero and Leander*, a passionate, tragic, comic fragment of an erotic epic. The poem is an adaptation of a late classical work by Musaeus; and its divided life is exemplified in its scholarly history. The earliest printed edition came from the press of Aldus Manutius in Venice, in 1494, which included the Greek text with a Latin translation—its printed history begins mediated through translation. The manuscript Aldus was working from identified the poem simply as the work of Musaeus, and Aldus therefore ascribed it to the legendary poet of that name, a pupil of Orpheus, and assumed it to be the most ancient classical poetry to survive—poetry, thus, in its purest, originary, form. And though throughout the next century there were many doubters concerning its antiquity, it was widely praised and often translated, again into Latin, and into various vernaculars (though not English). Julius Caesar Scaliger, in his early sixteenth-century *Poetics*, notoriously preferred it to Homer, and maintained that if Musaeus had written the *Iliad* and *Odyssey*, they would have been better poems. But after the great scholar Isaac Casaubon, late in the century, demonstrated that stylistically the poem could not, in fact, be early, but was clearly a work of the fifth century AD (its poet is appropriately called, in a number of other early manuscripts, not Musaeus but Musaeus the Grammarian), interest in it gradually subsided. The character of the poem thus went from radical innocence to oversophistication in a very few decades.

It is customary to praise Marlowe's scholarly achievement in *Hero and Leander* by observing how accurately it captures the high rhetorical flashiness of Musaeus's style, but the style of the original is far more artificial and literary. There is no match in Musaeus for Marlowe's enthusiasm. Marlowe's excitement may be the expression of his sense of the adolescence of poetry itself; but clearly this is a classic he is having a great deal of fun with. When, after Marlowe's death, George Chapman undertook to complete Marlowe's fragment, it became much more serious.

Hero and Leander is very daring, in many of the ways *Doctor Faustus* is. Like *Faustus*, it tempts the Renaissance reader with his deepest desires—the reader is in this case surely assumed to be male. If *Faustus* condemns blasphemy, the play nevertheless realizes or embodies it, presenting blasphemy on stage. *Hero and Leander* is a secular version of that Faustian presumptuousness, and all the blasphemy is sexual. The hero and heroine are incredibly, miraculously, outrageously beautiful, constantly being compared to the most perfect things imaginable, gods and goddesses, jewels, works of art, and coming out ahead. The god Apollo courted Hero ("for her hair"); Cupid himself pined for her, and mistook her for Venus; Leander was more beautiful than Endymion or Ganymede, his hair was more wonderful than the Golden Fleece, and so forth. A world of allusion and poetic elaboration is invoked to adorn these two; the poem, the style, the rhetoric, impose on the lovers a dangerous case of hubris. None of this comes from Musaeus.

One of the most striking aspects of the poem is its overt sexuality. There are Italian poems like this, but almost none in English until the next century; it is emotionally very daring. It is also very open about its sexual interests—the tradition that says that Marlowe was gay gets a good deal of support from *Hero and Leander.* Both lovers are described as infinitely desirable; but the praise of Leander is much more frankly sexual than that of Hero, and specifically homosexual. Gods and men pine away for Hero, but the measure of Leander's beauty is not that women desire him, but that men do: "Jove might have sipped out nectar from his hand"—he is as desirable as Ganymede; had Hippolytus seen him he would have abandoned his chastity; "The barbarous Thracian soldier, moved with naught, / Was moved with him, and for his favor sought": rough trade solicits him. Again, none of this comes from Musaeus, where Leander is not described. Hero is beautiful, Leander is all desire, the validation of her beauty.

Marlowe is certainly daring, though less so in a Renaissance context than he seems now; for adult men to be attracted to good-looking youths was quite conventional. Still, there is no way of arguing that it is merely conventional, that Marlowe does not really mean it, or does not mean it the way it sounds. The first sestiad includes a teasing description of how beautiful Leander's body is—

> I could tell ye
> How smooth his breast was, and how white his belly,
> And whose immortal fingers did imprint
> That heavenly path, with many a curious dint,
> That runs along his back

and the second sestiad has an extraordinary passage about Neptune making passes at Leander as he swims the Hellespont.

> He clapped his plump cheeks, with his tresses played,
> And smiling wantonly, his love bewrayed.
> He watched his arms, and as they opened wide
> At every stroke, betwixt them would he slide

And steal a kiss, and then run out and dance,
And as he turned, cast many a lustful glance,
And threw him gaudy toys to please his eye,
And dive into the water, and there pry
Upon his breast, his thighs, and every limb,
And up again, and close beside him swim,
And talk of love.

There is no indication that Marlowe feels, or expects his readers to feel, any anxiety over the enthusiastic depiction of a man making love to another man. Marlowe gets away with this partly because the subject is classical—"Greek" love—but partly too because sexuality in the period was simply much more undifferentiated than it is now. Neptune's lust for Leander in this context is neither abnormal nor shocking, though it is certainly comic. Leander's reaction—"You are deceived, I am no woman, I"—is more an indication of his sexual naivete than of his straightness.

Marlowe's poem is the best expression of the Ovidian world view in English. It is hyperbolic in much the same way Renaissance tragedy is; its heroes are braver or more beautiful than we are, and they are capable of more suffering; more is lost when they die; they provide us with the exemplary instances of passion against which ours are to be measured. The other side of the enthusiasm and overt sexuality is the sense of foreboding that also fills the poem, a sense that these heroes are too good for their world, that the gods are jealous, that nothing this beautiful is ever allowed to get away with it. The undercurrent of tragedy is always there, but Marlowe handles the moral issues in a characteristically subversive way. The tragedy we know is coming never qualifies the sensuality—the point is not that Hero and Leander ought not to be behaving this way. Quite the contrary: the point is that our world is simply not good enough for its heroes. Marlowe deals with the necessary tragic conclusion by omitting it, not finishing the poem. This is a work designed to be a fragment—another thing about it that is "classical."

The most subversive of Marlowe's subjects is how you get away with pleasure, and omitting the conclusion, the punishment for the lovers'—and the readers'—enjoyment is a neat way of cheating the moralists. Ironically, but also significantly, the poem was completed by the most moral and moralistic of Marlowe's contemporaries, George Chapman: two editions of *Hero and Leander* appeared in 1598, the second of which included Chapman's continuation. Chapman was an immensely learned and philosophical poet; but the kinship he felt with Marlowe was not based only on the fact that both were classicists. In Chapman's continuation, the lovers are perfect, but their love is unsanctified because they are unmarried; the goddess Juno, patron of marriage, has been neglected. They rectify the omission by sacrificing to Juno and formally marrying, but Venus is their true patron, not Juno, and the fates hate Venus and are jealous of the lovers' beauty and perfection; this time Leander crossing the Hellespont drowns, and Hero dies of grief. Chapman's style is quite different from Marlowe's, but his admiration for Marlowe is clear, and he has his own kind of power and pathos. At the conclusion of the poem, the lovers are metamorphosed into goldfinches:

> Neptune for pity in his arms did take them,
> Flung them into the air, and did awake them
> Like two sweet birds . . .
> . . . .
> And so most beautiful their colors show,
> As none (so little) like them: her sad brow
> A sable velvet feather covers quite,
> Even like the forehead-cloths that in the night,
> Or when they sorrow, ladies use to wear;
> Their wings, blue, red, and yellow, mixed appear;
> Colors that, as we construe colors, paint
> Their states to life; the yellow shows their saint,
> The devil Venus, left them; blue, their truth;
> The red and black, ensigns of death and ruth.
> And this true honor from their love-deaths sprung,
> They were the first that ever poet sung.

"Their saint / The devil Venus" is a good indication of how divided Chapman's moral imagination is here. The point is not, obviously, to blame the lovers for falling in love; it is that the distinction between saint and devil is discernable only in hindsight. When Chapman subsequently revised the poem, he had second thoughts about even this, and "the devil Venus" became "the dainty Venus"—both delicately beautiful and fastidious or reluctant, but no longer damnable.

The most extraordinary thing about Chapman's continuation is that this moralist wants to be associated with the work of Marlowe at all: when he was murdered in 1593, Marlowe was under investigation for atheism, blasphemy, counterfeiting (all that is missing is sodomy, and the charges hover dangerously close to that too)—in short, universal subversion. But Chapman saw a different Marlowe, his life, like the poem, passionate and tragically incomplete. Similarly, when Shakespeare quotes Marlowe in *As You Like It*: "Dead shepherd, now I feel thy saw of might, / Whoever loved that loved not at first sight?" (3.5.81–82; compare *Hero and Leander* 1.176)—it is as the model of the innocent wisdom of love. Chapman's and Shakespeare's Marlowe is the fictitious Musaeus, the primal poet. Chapman's continuation appears to the modern reader very different in character from Marlowe's fragment. The seventeenth-century reader would have found the differences less striking, and there is no evidence that Chapman's addition was ever considered either inappropriate or unworthy. It immediately established itself as an integral part of the poem, and was invariably reprinted with it until well into the twentieth century.

Cultural Politics

If Marlowe modeled his career on the transgressive Ovid, Spenser saw himself as an English Virgil, beginning with pastoral and maturing into the epic of empire. He too is radically new, though not least (like Stanyhurst) by preserving, or reinventing, archaism: *The Faerie Queene* is indebted as much to the moderns Ariosto and Tasso as to Chaucer, but it employs a pseudo-Chaucerian vocabulary. Spenser had done something similar in *The Shepheardes Calender*. There the language was claimed to be both rustic and authentically English, both speaking as real shepherds speak and restoring words that had been "cleane disherited"—an appeal to sociology, anthropology, and linguistic archeology. The language of *The Faerie Queene* is just as clearly an invented one, designed, like its fable of knights and dragons, to give the air of antiquity. Spenser explained in his *Letter to Sir Walter Ralegh* that he wanted to avoid "the envie, and suspicion of present time."[12] Ben Jonson was unimpressed, asserting in *Timber or Discoveries*, his commonplace book, that "Spenser, in affecting the ancients, writ no language."[13] For Jonson, affecting the ancients was a vice, if the ancients were English. Affecting the classics, however, was obviously a virtue.

But what classics? Julius Caesar Scaliger preferred Musaeus to Homer; Stanyhurst maintained that the only true Latin classics were Virgil in the *Aeneid* and Ovid in the *Metamorphoses*: "As for Ennius, Horace, Juvenal, Persius, and thee rablement of such cheate [fraudulent] Poëtes, theyre dooinges are, for favoure of antiquitye, rather to be pacientlye allowed thean highlye regarded."[14] Jonson's admiration for Martial, Marlowe's and Milton's for Lucan, are an indication of how narrowly or broadly construed the classic could be, and how dependent the definition was on personal tastes. Even for Erasmus, the classic required much interpretation and redirection to make it accord with humanist ideology. Of Virgil's openly homoerotic second Eclogue, sung by the shepherd Corydon hopelessly in love with the handsome slave-boy Alexis, Erasmus writes that schoolmasters should teach the poem "as a parable of unstable friendship. . . . Alexis is of the town, Corydon a countryman; Corydon a shepherd, Alexis a man of society; Alexis cultivated, young, graceful, Corydon rude, crippled, his youth far behind him. Hence the impossibility of a true friendship. The lesson finally left on the mind of the pupil is that it is the prudent part to choose friends among those whose tastes and characters agree with our own. Such methods of treating a classical story, by forcing attention to the moral to be deduced from it, will serve to counteract any harm which a more literal interpretation might possibly convey."[15] Literal interpretation is dangerous; meaning is endlessly malleable to produce the desired moral; students who read for themselves turn out like Marlowe. And though the text here remains intact, outright expurgation was common enough, for example in editions of Martial and Juvenal.

What then are our obligations to the classical cultures we are appropriating? The metaphor of theft is pervasive throughout the age, but it is deployed without any moral implications—the French humanist Joachim du Bellay's term for rectifying and enriching the vernacular through imitating the classics is even starker: *piller*, plunder. Montaigne employs the conceit of cultural pillage but disarms it by comparing the act to the collection of pollen by bees: "*les abeilles pillotent deça delà les fleurs*." John Florio's Jacobean translation softens the metaphor further: in English, bees do not plunder but "sucke this, and cull that flower."[16] The modern metaphor, "borrow," seemingly avoids the elements of larceny and violence, but is surely merely a euphemism for theft: is there any means of repaying this loan? By introducing bees into the metaphor, Montaigne renders it fiscally responsible: when bees plunder plants, they are also pollinating them.

Sir Thomas More makes humanist theft the subject of a witty epigram, *Ad Gallum Sublegentem Veterum Carmina*, "To a Frenchman Stealing the Poetry of the Ancients":

> Frenchman, surely you in our time have the same wit and
> inspiration
> that ancient poets had, for you write the same poems, and
> frequently
> word for word.[17]

But is this really an attack on some anonymous Frenchman? Or is the epigram perhaps a way for More to distinguish himself as a poet from all the poetasters who shall remain nameless, even from that whole nation of poetasters across the Channel, the defining feature of poetasters being that they have no wit of their own and therefore steal the wit of others? The trouble is, however, that the defining feature of humanist poetry is precisely how closely and accurately it replicates that of the ancients. Perhaps the epigram is not really a francophobic barb, but a sly joke about humanism itself, the thieving Frenchman as the *reductio ad absurdum* of the humanist ideal. Perhaps—but perhaps not: many of More's own epigrams are direct translations from the Greek Anthology; sometimes this is acknowledged, sometimes not. More surely would say that any properly educated humanist will recognize the poems as homage, not theft; but so, doubtless, would the felonious Frenchman. Whatever humanism conceives theft or plunder to be here, nothing about it is viewed as criminal or destructive; but there is also no recognition that in remaking our own culture through a highly selective imitation, we misrepresent and remake classical culture.

For most English readers, the classics were filtered through translation—necessarily in the case of Greek, which was less widely taught, but also in the case of Latin, despite the fact that Latin permeated the school system, and that insofar as literature was taught, it consisted of the Latin classics. Nevertheless, there was an increasing market for translation: Latin literacy, and the refined taste it implied, in fact did not descend very far down the social scale. Remember Tottel deploring "the rude skill of common ears"—those ears belonged to a substantial proportion of the readers he was undertaking to attract. Sir Thomas More notoriously said that if he ever found any of his works translated into English he would burn them,[18] to prevent their being read by the wrong people—the uneducated, and also implicitly Protestants, those who required vernacular translations of the Vulgate. The wrong people, whether heretical or merely ignorant, were defined by their inadequate knowledge of Latin. Moreover, the education of readers could never be taken for granted. The 1613 edition of Joshua Sylvester's translation of Du Bartas's *Divine Weekes*, by that time an English classic, includes a glossary explaining "hard words." By far the largest number are proper names from classical history and myth, including Achilles, Hercules, Oedipus ("a Riddle-Reader of Thebes"), Parnassus, Pluto, Ulysses, Vulcan. Even the literate classes needed help.

Thomas Phaer wrote, in an explanatory note to the first segment of his *Aeneid* translation,

"Thus farfourth good readers, aswell for defence of my country language (which I have heard discommended of manye, and estemed of some to be more than barbarous) as also for honest recreation of you the nobilitie, gentlemen and Ladies that study not Latyne, I have taken some travaile to expresse this most excellent writer."[19]

Philemon Holland in 1601 offered a more detailed apologia for his translation of Pliny's *Historia Naturalis*, an argument from common sense with a palpable tone of defensiveness.

> And yet some there be so grosse as to give out, That these and such like books ought not to be published in the vulgar tongue. It is a shame (quoth one) that Livie speaketh English as hee doth: Latinists onely are to bee acquainted with him: As who would say, the souldiour were to have recourse unto the universitie for militarie skill and knowledge; or the schollar to put on arms and pitch a campe. What should Plinie (saith another) bee read in English, and the mysteries couched in his books divulged: as if the husbandman, the mason, carpenter, goldsmith, painter, lapidarie, and engraver, with other artificers, were bound to seeke unto great clearks or linguists for instructions in their severall arts. Certes, such Momi as these, besides their blind and erroneous opinion, thinke not so honourably of their native countrey and mother tongue as they ought: who if they were so well affected that way as they should be, would wish rather and endeavour by all means to triumph now over the Romans in subduing their literature under the dent of the English pen, in requitall of the conquest sometime over this Island, atchieved by the edge of their sword. As for our speech, was not Latine as common and naturall in Italie, as English here with us. And if Plinie faulted not but deserved well of the Romane name, in laying abroad the riches and hidden treasures of Nature, in that Dialect or Idiome which was familiar to the basest clowne: why should any man be blamed for enterprising the semblable, to the commodotie of that countrey in which and for which he was borne. Are we the onely nation under heaven unworthie to tast of such knowledge? Or is our language so barbarous, that it will not admit in proper tearms a forrein phrase? I honour them in my heart, who having of late daies troden the way before me in Plutarch, Tacitus, and others, have made good proofe, that as the tongue in an English mans head is framed so flexible and obsequent, that it can pronounce naturally any other language; so a pen in his hand is able sufficiently to expresse Greeke, Latine, and Hebrew.[20]

For Holland, the classics are useful and informative, and ought to be available to anyone literate; but he assumes that only "great clerks or linguists" will be able to read them in Latin. Similarly, Caesar's *De Bello Gallico*, that classic of both military history and introductory Latin prose, was not left to the Latin of schoolchildren. William Cecil commissioned an English version from Arthur Golding at the same time that Golding was composing his Ovid. Both were, in fact, unlikely projects for Golding. All his many other translations were of contemporary religious or historical works, and as a staunch Calvinist, he warned against reading Ovid for mere pleasure, and duly supplied the fables with moralizations. Caesar did not require moralization, but he did require translation.

Golding's Caesar

Golding was a tireless proselytizer for Protestant doctrine: he published translations of six works of Calvin, as well as of two extensive Lutheran commentaries on the New Testament, and about a dozen other theological works, including, in 1587, *A woorke concerning the trewnesse of the Christian religion, written in French: against atheists, Epicures, Paynims, Jewes, Mahumetists, and other infidels. By Philip of Mornay Lord of Plessie Marlie. Begunne to be translated into English by Sir Philip Sidney Knight, and at his request finished by Arthur Golding.* Clearly he was much in demand for both his knowledge of Latin and French and his commitment to Protestant theology.

The translation of Caesar's *De Bello Gallico* was undertaken at Cecil's request at the outset of Queen Elizabeth's reign, when he was her secretary of state. Golding and Cecil had for several years been closely connected. Golding's half-sister had married the Earl of Oxford, and his brother Henry was Oxford's steward. When the earl died, Oxford's son became Cecil's ward; Arthur, the boy's uncle, was a member of the household, and lived in Cecil House for several years. Cecil had given Golding a partial translation of Caesar by John Brende, requesting that Golding, who had already published several translations from Latin, complete it—there was, at this point, no complete English translation of Caesar.

The project had been a logical one for John Brende (ca. 1515–1559), who under Henry VIII and Edward VI had served as a surveyor of fortifications in the north of England, and had been active in their repair and redesign. A logistical expert, he was sent on several trips to the continent to procure munitions, and was active in the negotiations relating to the war with Scotland in 1547–1549—he would have been thoroughly familiar with Caesar's classic treatise on the art of war. As an agent of Protector Somerset under Edward VI, he was imprisoned in the Tower at Somerset's fall, but was released after a few months, probably at the instigation of John, Duke of Northumberland, protector after Somerset; and Brende clearly saw Northumberland as a patron.

Edward VI's will provided that he should be succeeded not by his half-sister Mary Tudor, eldest child of Henry VIII, who had been named next in the line of succession under the will of Henry VIII, but by Lady Jane Grey, Henry VIII's niece and the daughter-in-law of Northumberland—Mary had remained a staunch Catholic, whereas Lady Jane was firmly Protestant, and would ensure the Protestant succession. Northumberland had doubtless been influential in the drafting of the will, and on Edward's death was instrumental in installing Lady Jane as queen. Mary, however, had not only popular support, but more important, that of the Privy Council, and after nine days Lady Jane was deposed, Mary declared queen; and Northumberland was arrested, found guilty of treason, and executed. His client John Brende promptly converted to Catholicism and became a loyal supporter of Queen Mary, serving again on the Scottish borders. His service continued after the accession of Elizabeth. He was clearly a faithful servant to whomever he served.

Brende was a serious scholar and an excellent Latinist; his translation of Quintus Curtius Rufus's *Historiae Alexandri Magni, The historie of Quintus Curcius conteyning the actes of the greate Alexander,* appeared in 1553. A translation of Caesar's *De Bello Gallico*, another classic model for the conduct of military enterprises, was a logical next project. At his death in 1559 he had reached book 5. William Cecil, who from the beginning of Elizabeth's reign was involved in a long-term systematic survey of England's defenses and preparedness, was the obvious patron for it, just as the military hero the Duke of Northumberland had been the dedicatee of Brende's translation of *The Actes of the Greate Alexander*.

Brende's dedicatory epistle to Northumberland gives a good sense of the utility of both history and translation for sixteenth-century England. To begin with, a knowledge of past events is valuable to everyone, but especially to those in authority: "For in them men may see the groundes and beginnynges of common wealthes, the causes of their encrease, of their prosperous mayntenaunce, and good preservation: and againe by what meanes they decreased, decayed, and came to ruyne" (Aii^{r}).[21] History, in Brende's view, teaches a firmly conservative ideology: "In histories it is apparent how dangerous it is to begin alterations in a commonwealth. How envy and hatredes oft risyng upon smal causes, have ben the destruction of great kyngdomes. And that disobeyers of hygher powers, and such as rebellyd agaynst magystrates, never escapyd punyshment, nor came to good end" (Aii$^{r–v}$).

Translation, therefore, is desirable because these lessons are useful not only for the learned and powerful:

> Seing histories be then so good and necessary, it were much requisite for men's instruccion, that they were translated into suche tongues as most men myght understand them: and specially the histories of antiquitye, whych both for the greatnes of the actes done in those daies and for the excellencie of the writers, have much majestye and many ensamples of vertue. I therfore havyng alwayes desired that we englishmen might be founde as forwarde in that behalfe as other nations, which have brought all worthie histories into their naturall language, did a fewe yeares paste attempte the translacion of Quintus Curtius. (Aiii^{v}–Aiv^{r})

As for the history of Alexander the Great, it is exemplary because this hero's life was distinguished by "a moost speciall providence and predestinacion of god: who prospered so his proceedinges that . . . he never encountred with eny enemyes whom he overcame not, he beseiged no citye that he wanne [won] not, nor assailed nation that he subdued not" (Aiv^{r}). Finally, the translation is dedicated to Northumberland "considering the qualities of your grace, which seme to have certeine affinitie and resemblaunce wyth such as were the very vertues in Alexander" (Aiv^{r}). The affinity with Alexander had obviously faded by the time the translation was published with its encomium—Northumberland was to be executed within three months.

At the time Brende undertook his translation of Caesar's *De Bello Gallico,* no complete translation into English existed. In 1530 William Rastell had published an anonymous translation from a French version of excerpts from books 4 and 5, constituting those sections relating to England—this, until the reign of Elizabeth I, was Caesar in English.[22] Nothing survives of Brende's five books that Cecil gave Golding. Golding says in his dedicatory epistle that he began by completing the remaining portion, but that he was persuaded to retranslate Brende's section "least I mighte have semed to seeke excuse of slouthfulnes, or to refuse paines [out] of wilfullnes, rather than to defend my selfe by unablenesse" (*ii^{v}).[23] Golding clearly wants to be in control of the whole book, and of how he appears as an author.

Golding's preface to his Caesar is far less high minded and philosophical than Brende's to Quintus Curtius, and indeed, Golding remarks at once that, unlike Brende, he is in no way qualified to undertake a version of this important military treatise, "considering mine own want of experience not only in matters of war, but also in divers other things wherof this history entreateth" (*ii^{r}). He has yielded to Cecil's "favorable encouragement," and merely undertakes to justify his unwillingness to complete the manuscript he was given, but rather to replace Brende's portion with a version of his own. As for the utility of ancient history, it is simply assumed; Golding's preface *To the Reader* is concerned not with justifying the project, but with summarizing the history of the Gallic lands after Caesar's time, thus bringing the work up to date. But the summary has a significant subtext: England's title to the crown of France is firmly asserted:

> No one Nation . . . hath so often and so sore afflicted theym as our Englishe Nation hath done: whose kinges divers times before, but specially from the time of King Edward the thyrd, have contended with theym, not so muche for anye one part or Province of the country, as for the substance of the crowne and possession of the whole Realme, descended to our kinges by ryghte of inheritance. And they have both gayned and hild [held] it many yeres, untill fortune chaunging her copye, hath transferred the possession again to the Frenchmen, the right remaynyng styl to the Crowne of England. (**ii$^{r–v}$)

For a work appearing at the beginning of Elizabeth's reign, these were fighting words, since the last English foothold in France, Calais, had been lost under Mary only seven years earlier, in 1558.

Caesar's prose is famously straightforward, direct, and relatively unadorned (hence it has become the standard introduction to Latin prose for two centuries of English-speaking schoolchildren). Golding's translation is an accurate reflection of the style. Unlike the Ovid translation, with its Puritan moralizations, there is no attempt to revise Caesar in the image of Elizabethan England; and of course, there is much less that needed to be revised. Golding makes small adjustments that one might call essentially cosmetic—for example, in the sections on the invasion of Britain, Caesar regularly refers to the natives as barbarians. Golding simply substitutes "Britons," but makes no attempt to mitigate the perfidiousness of their dealings with the Romans, which, in any case, Golding probably considered admirable: Caesar was, after all, an invader.

There is a great deal of critical commentary on Golding's Ovid, but almost none on his Caesar, or indeed, any of his other works. In his own time, he was praised as a poet, and for his religious fervor in domesticating essential works of Protestant doctrine. The only full biography, by his descendent L. T. Golding, *An Elizabethan Puritan: Arthur Golding, the Translator of Ovid's Metamorphoses and also of John Calvin's Sermons* (1937), claims that, like the Ovid, Golding's Caesar was "warmly received," but this is going beyond the evidence. That there was a continuing demand for the book is clear from the fact that a second edition appeared in 1590. That it had established itself as the standard translation of this important work is evident merely from the fact that no other translation was found necessary or desirable in the period. By the turn of the century, however, the book starts to look less essential. In 1600, Clement Edmondes published his *Observations upon Caesars Commentaries*, reissued in 1604 with his own abridged translation of books 1–5—Caesar was a book for use; one could be selective. This was published again in 1609. Edmondes did a complete translation of the Latin text, but this was not published until 1655; Edmondes had died in 1622. For almost a century, readers who wanted Caesar complete in English read Golding.

L. T. Golding's 1937 biography cites striking evidence of the survival of the book's prestige into the nineteenth century. In Longfellow's poetic romance about the Plymouth Colony, *The Courtship of Miles Standish* (1858), Standish, the military adviser to the Puritan immigrants in Massachusetts, has a small but imposing library:

> Fixed to the opposite wall was a shelf of books, and among them
> Prominent three, distinguished alike for bulk and for binding;
> Bariffe's Artillery Guide, and the Commentaries of Caesar
> Out of the Latin translated by Arthur Goldinge of London,
> And, as if guarded by these, between them was standing the Bible.[24]

Bariffe's Artillery Guide is William Barriffe's *Military discipline: or, The young artillery man. Wherein is discoursed and showne the postures both of musket and pike* [. . .], published in 1635. Longfellow imagining the essential guides in the life of a seventeenth-century professional soldier places Golding's Caesar beside the basic handbook of artillery practice and the Bible. This is a nice piece of dramatic detail; it is, however, historically impossible: since the action of the poem takes place shortly after the founding of the Plymouth colony in 1620, Standish could have had a copy of Golding, but not yet of Barriffe. Moreover, the three volumes would certainly not have been "alike for bulk." Barriffe is a hefty quarto, Caesar a well-proportioned octavo, and both would have been considerably smaller than any Bible. Longfellow knew Golding's Caesar by reputation. It seems unlikely that he had ever seen a copy.

Sources and Resources

Surely such examples imply that the extent of Latin literacy in early modern England, even among the educated, has been greatly overstated. The Greek classics posed even greater problems than the Latin ones. I have already cited North's Plutarch and Arthur Hall's *Iliad*, based on French translations, and Chapman's Homer on a Latin one; but a more striking case is George Gascoigne and Francis Kinwelmersh's *Jocasta*, a version of Euripides's *Phoenician Women*, the first Greek play to be published in English. The authors do certainly purport to be translating Euripides—their title reads *Jocasta: A Tragedie writtein in Greeke by Euripides. Translated and digested into Acte, by George Gascoigne and Francis Kinwelmersh*—though in fact they are working quite faithfully from a recent Italian version by Lodovico Dolce.

Gascoigne and Kinwelmersh do not follow Dolce in one respect: Dolce says nothing whatever about Euripides—his *Giocasta* purports to be his own, though he acknowledges in a dedication that he has taken "le inventioni, le sentenze, e la testura" (the texture, the general feel) "dagli antichi," from the ancients.[25] In fact, Dolce's indebtedness is far more complex than the English translators', and Euripides comes to him through several intermediaries. Dolce's Latin was fluent, but he knew little Greek. He used a recent Latin translation of *The Phoenician Women*, and his *Giocasta* is a free version of the play, omitting scenes and adding others, heavily reliant on Seneca's *Phoenissae*.[26] And while a fulsome dedication praises his patron's knowledge of Greek and Latin, there is no suggestion that he will recognize in *Giocasta* Euripides's (or Seneca's) *Phoenician Women*.

Perhaps all this implies is that Italian humanism felt more at home with the ancients than the British latecomers did, saw themselves as part of a continuous tradition, and therefore more free to adapt and appropriate the classics. But by the end of the century, English writers like Marlowe, Chapman, and Jonson (to say nothing of such programmatic classicists as William Gager and Thomas Watson) were quite at home with the ancient models, and not at all constrained by them—think of *Hero and Leander*. There probably were vernacular poets as good at ancient Greek as Marlowe, but surely nobody had so much fun with it. Marlowe, Chapman, and Jonson were exceptional, certainly, and there is obviously condescension in Jonson's notorious allusion to Shakespeare's "small Latin and less Greek": Jonson was very proud of his learning. But it also testifies to the fact that in Elizabethan England, even provincial grammar school boys studied both Latin and Greek, and had a taste for the classics, though they might not be sufficiently fluent to read them with ease. Most English writers worked the way Gascoigne and Kinwelmersh—and Shakespeare—did, making use of translations and modern paraphrases to gain access to the ancient texts.

Our attitude toward that freedom has been on the whole dismissive—we prize originality, and plagiarism has been a favorite charge of modern scholars against Renaissance classicism. Modern critics are usually willing to allow Renaissance authors their sources provided they are sufficiently ancient. If Gascoigne and Kinwelmersh had gone to Seneca for *Jocasta*, rather than to Lodovico Dolce, the fact probably would not have been a strike against them. Even with classical sources, however, the idea of intermediate texts disturbs us. Here is a single example: E. W. Talbert, a scholar of Renaissance reference works, discovered that Ben Jonson's learned marginal annotations, such as those to *The Masque of Queens* and *Sejanus*, are often copied directly from dictionaries and encyclopedias. Talbert felt that Jonson's learning was thereby impugned. He accused the poet of lying when he claims, in the dedicatory epistle to the masque, that he wrote the work "out of the fullness and memory of my former readings."[27] To anyone who knew anything about Jonson, the accusation was nonsense—dozens of Greek and Latin texts from Jonson's library survive, with copious annotations in Jonson's hand; but as a poet constantly short of cash, he repeatedly sold off his books. When necessary, he used whatever reference works were available, including dictionaries and encyclopedias. Every age has its reference books, and a more scrupulous generation than ours may criticize us for failing to acknowledge our use of bibliographies and periodical indexes—to say nothing of Google and Wikipedia—as if we were thereby pretending to carry all the relevant scholarship in our heads.

Chapter 3

The Sound of Classical

Meter and Rhyme

Consider some samples, for the most part in modernized texts for ease of comparison. Here is a bit of Surrey's "strange meter," Dido preparing for death:

> Sweet spoils, whiles God and destinies it would,
> Receive this sprite, and rid me of these cares:
> I lived and ran the course fortune did grant;
> And under earth my great ghost now shall wend:
> A goodly town I built, and saw my walls;
> Happy, alas, too happy, if these coasts
> The Troyan ships had never touchèd aye.

In the 1550s this would have sounded strange, though it retains some bits of traditional alliterative verse ("sweet spoils," "great ghost").

Now here is a passage from the opening of Thomas Phaer's *Aeneid*:

> Of arms, and of the man of Troy, that first by fatal flight
> Did thence arrive to Lavine land that now Italia hight,

> But shaken sore with many a storm by seas and land ytost
> And all for Juno's endless wrath that wrought to have had him lost,
> And sorrows great in wars he bode ere he the walls could frame
> Of mighty Rome . . .

Today Phaer has disappeared from the literary histories, but this really reads quite impressively, a supple verse rhythm with real momentum. This is what English Virgil sounded like for Elizabethan readers.

Here is the same passage from Richard Stanyhurst's quantitative *Aeneid*, 1582.

> I blaze the captain first from Troy city repairing,
> Like wand'ring pilgrim to famoused Italy trudging,
> And coast of Lavin': soused with tempestuous hurlwind,
> On land and sailing, by God's predestinate order:
> But chief through Juno's long fost'red deadly revengement.

Here it is in the original orthography:

> I blaze thee captayne first from Troy cittye repairing,
> Lyke wandring pilgrim too famosed Italie trudging,
> And coast of Lavyn: soust wyth tempestuus hurlwynd,
> On land and sayling, bi Gods predestinat order:
> But chiefe through Junoes long fostred deadlye revengement.

If you count this out you can see that it really is quantitative, though there was some fiddling with the spelling to make it work—'cittye' has to have a double t to make the i long, 'to' has a double o to make it long, 'by' is spelled 'bi' to make it short, etc. For the London edition of the next year, the publisher regularized the spelling, thus defeating the quantitative scheme (he either missed the point, or didn't care). The book was not reissued; obviously, it met with little success. Even this brief passage has undeniable awkwardnesses ("soused with tempestuous hurlwind"); rhythmically, however, it is natural enough, though the end-stopped lines slow it down.

Here in 1601, only nineteen years but an aesthetic generation later, is Ben Jonson in *Poetaster*. The emperor Augustus asks Virgil to recite a bit of the *Aeneid*, his work in progress. Dido and Aeneas take shelter in the storm:

fire and air did shine,
As guilty of the match; and from the hill
The nymphs with shriekings do the region fill.
Here first began their bane; this day was ground
Of all their ills; for now, nor rumour's sound,
Nor nice respect of state, moves Dido ought;
Her love no longer now by stealth is sought: (5.2.65–71)

This is an English Virgil we can recognize as classical. Not that one would mistake it for Dryden or Pope—there is no playfulness; it has a formality and stiffness that are part of the Jonsonian sense of authority. But in 1601, on Jonson's stage, Virgil no longer sounds early-modern.

Jonson himself reveals that he was not the catalyst. In the first act of *Poetaster*, Ovid recites one of his *Amores*. The lines Jonson gives him are substantially the translation done a decade before by Marlowe.[1] Marlowe's *Ovids Elegies*—the first translation into English—had been published surreptitiously in 1599, in a volume with John Davies's epigrams. The book, as we have seen, had been banned; but Marlowe—notorious atheist, "epicure," counterfeiter—was already the classical benchmark. His Ovid was in pentameter couplets: for Jonson in 1601, that was the prosody of classical poetry, not Phaer's or Golding's fourteeners, and least of all Surrey's blank verse. Blank verse for Jonson was a vehicle not for classical epic, but for the play itself, dramatic dialogue—poetry comes in couplets, but speech on the English stage, starting in the 1560s, and from the 1580s on, is predominantly blank verse.

Here, for comparison with the *Aeneid* samples, is Golding's *Metamorphoses*. In Book 10, Venus learns of the death of Adonis:

Dame Venus in her chariot drawn with swans was scarce arrived
At Cyprus, when she knew afar the sigh of him deprived
Of life. She turned her cygnets back, and when she from the sky

> Beheld him dead, and in his blood beweltred for to lie:
> She leapèd down, . . .

Rhythmically secure, it reads aloud impressively (Ezra Pound called it the most beautiful book in English), and though it seems to speak with the voice of a much earlier era, it was in fact written within Marlowe's lifetime.

The Debate over Quantity

Roger Ascham, writing in the 1560s, in the course of a treatise on education, urged the reform of English poetry on classical models: "our English tong, in avoyding barbarous ryming, may as well receive right quantitie of sillables, and true order of versifying . . . as either Greeke or Latin."[2] He cites as an example of right quantity of syllables and true order of versifying this translation by the scholar and poet William Watson of a verse from the *Odyssey*:

> All travelers do gladly report great prayse of Ulysses.
> For that he knew many mens maners, and saw many Cities.

This does not sound much like English poetry, but if we count it out we can see that it does, more or less, follow the Latin quantitative rules. The trouble is that the rules have little to do with English pronunciation. Vowels are long by position (followed by two consonants) regardless of how they are pronounced; moreover, Watson makes vowels long if they are stressed (such as the *a* in "travelers" and "manners" and the *i* in "cities"), again regardless of how they are pronounced. For the Elizabethans, this was a problem not with the rules, but with English, both in its dissimilarity from the classical tongues and in the variety of spelling and pronunciation at the time—proponents of quantitative verse in English observe that a necessary first step would be to stabilize the language, as Gabriel Harvey wrote to Edmund Spenser, "there is no one more regular and justifiable direction, eyther for the assured and infallible Certaintie of our English Artificiall Prosodye particularly, or generally to bring our Language into Arte and to frame a Grammer or Rhetorike thereof, than first of all universally to agree upon one and the same ortographie."[3]

But even with a stable orthography, the application of quantitative rules to English is problematic. To begin with, it is not clear in what sense an English vowel can be said to be long or short—to consider the vowels in stressed syllables invariably long, as Watson does, is entirely arbitrary. There is obviously a difference between the *a* sound in 'rat' and in 'rate'; such vowels are now described as short and long, but in pronunciation, they may or may not be of equal extension: thus, the *a* in 'rate' is not, in speaking, longer than the *a* in 'rat,' it is simply pronounced differently; whereas the *i* in 'rise' is certainly longer than the *i* in 'rid.' If quantity means length, English vowels are too erratic to serve—Harvey observed to Spenser that in some quantitative hexameters Spenser had sent him, "the," "ye" and "he" were treated as short, but "me" was long.[4] The issue is especially vexed in the case of vowels that are long by position. The most common examples in English are the -ing endings of participles, which are invariably unaccented and stubbornly short when spoken. In fact, Thomas Campion confronted precisely this problem; and his way of dealing with it gives a clear sense of how willed the whole quantitative system in English necessarily was: "For though we accent the second [syllable] of *Trumpington* short, yet is it naturally long, and so of necessity must be held of every composer."[5] What can "naturally" mean here? Are the rules of Latin prosody laws of nature? Campion might have felt that the case could be argued, just as Julius Caesar Scaliger asserted in his *Poetics* that though the function of poetry was to imitate nature, we can best imitate nature by imitating Virgil.[6] Harvey, however, had a clear sense of the practical problems, writing to Spenser, "in short, this is the very short and long: position neither maketh short nor long in our tongue," and concludes that some other rule must be found for English "that should as universally and canonically hold amongst us as position doth with the Latins and Greeks."[7]

The larger assumption behind Ascham's and Harvey's proposals for a new poetry was that the "barbarous" English of the time could be rectified by the application of classical rules. Thus John Hall (writing, needless to say, in English) deplores the decline of Latin and Greek:

> Since pedling *Barbarismes* gan be in request,
> Nor classicke tongues, nor learning found no rest.[8]

A return to the classics held out the promise of culture and civility—not only in poetry, of course, but poetry seemed a particularly clear example. Nobody thought the transformation would be easy; a hectoring and bullying tone is common throughout the discussion. But for a brief moment the classical rules, with their formality and dignity, seemed the wave of the future for English verse, rescuing it from the crudeness, and the sheer popularity, of the native tradition.

From our perspective, the whole quantitative project seems dead in the water, but Thomas Nashe took it seriously enough to launch a vitriolic attack on Stanyhurst for presuming to compete with Phaer's *Aeneid,* which for Nashe is an English classic.[9] In fact, Stanyhurst in his preface is full of praise for Phaer's translation; he offers his version as an example of what English verse would be if it were properly classical, following Ascham's and Harvey's precepts. Nevertheless, the verse of Stanyhurst's *Aeneid* was declared by Nashe to be "hexameter furie," and he parodied it in the preface to Robert Greene's *Menaphon*:

> Then did he make, heavens vault to rebounde with rounce robble hobble
> Of ruffe raffe roaring, with thwick thwack thurlery bouncing.[10]

This is obviously overstated for effect, but in fact, not by much. Here is Stanyhurst on Vulcan's forge, a passage from Book 8 appended to the translation of the first four books:

> Under is a kennel, wheare Chymneys fyrye be scorching
> Of *Cyclopan* tosters, with rent rocks chamferye sharded,
> Lowd dub a dub tabering with frapping rip rap of *Aetna*.
> (sig. *O*1^{v}–*O*2^{r})

Nashe's ridicule is in the service of an invidious comparison with Phaer's fourteeners, which are declared magnificent. Phaer is the norm, and Stanyhurst is accused of malice in presuming to displace him. Judging from the parody, the animus is directed not at Stanyhurst's quantitative system, but at both his alliteration (in fact, except for occasional admittedly exaggerated onomatopoeic effects, Stanyhurst's verse is not notably alliterative), and especially what Nashe takes to be the rhythmical overaccentuation of the verse—"foule lumbring boystrous wallowing measures."[11] Indeed, one of the problems with quantitative verse in English is negotiating the stresses—English is an accentual language (so is Latin, but in Latin stress and quantity are generally not in conflict). It is not even clear that Nashe understood that the hexameters were quantitative. Nor, probably, did the English publisher Henry Bynneman, despite his inclusion of Stanyhurst's prefatory dedication explaining the system: as we have seen, in order to indicate quantity, for the 1582 Leiden edition Stanyhurst had introduced doubled vowels and diphthongs, producing an orthography that was, even by the loose standards of Elizabethan spelling, distinctly eccentric. Bynneman, redoing the volume in London the next year, systematically normalized the spelling, with the result that it no longer served as a guide to the verse's properly classical rhythm, nor did the verse accord with Stanyhurst's account of it in the preface. What was in effect the translation's principal point, its most powerful justification, was thereby removed.

Nevertheless, Stanyhurst's meter was still a live issue at the turn of the century—here is the satirist John Hall again in 1599:

> Another scorns the home-spun thred of rimes,
> Match'd with the loftie feete of elder times:
> Giue me the numbred verse that *Virgill* sung,
> And *Virgill* selfe shall speake the English toung:
> *Manhood and garboiles shall he chaunt* with changed feete
> And head-strong *Dactils* making Music meete.
> The nimble *Dactils* striuing to out-go
> The drawling *Spondees* pacing it below.
> The lingring Spondees, labouring to delay,
> The breath-lesse Dactils with a sodaine stay.
> Who euer saw a Colte wanton and wilde,
> Yoakt with a slow-foote Oxe on fallow field?
> Can right areed how handsomely besets
> Dull Spondees with the English Dactilets?

Hall then echoes Nashe's strictures on Stanyhurst's rhythmical excesses, and adds a couplet attacking his neologisms:

> If *Jove* speake English in a thundring cloud,
> *Thwick thwack,* and *Riffe raffe*, rores he out aloud.
> Fie on the forged mint that did create
> New coyne of words never articulate.[12]

Clearly Hall notices a good deal more than Nashe, and it is only in hindsight that he seems to be beating a dead horse—Campion's *Observations in the Art of English Poesie,* promoting the quantitative system and attacking the use of rhyme, was published in 1602, and was answered in 1603 by Samuel Daniel's *Defence of Ryme.*

Stanyhurst's own account of his poetic revisionism is both defensive and accurate about the problems it raises. He is fully aware that the Latin rules are not really adaptable to English; he observes, moreover, that they are not even fully adaptable to Latin:

> For in as much as thee Latins have not been authors of theese verses [i.e., were not the originators of the rules], but traced in thee steps of thee Greekes, why should we with thee stringes of thee Latin rules cramp oure tongue more than the Latins doe fetter theyre speeche, as yt were wyth thee chaynes of thee Greeke preceptes. Also that nature wyl not permit us too fashion oure wordes in all poinctes correspondent too thee Latinistes, may easely appeere in suche termes as we borrow of theym. For example: the first of *Breviter* is short, thee first of *briefly* wyth us must be long.[13]

But Stanyhurst's revisionism went well beyond the quantitative scheme. He came from an old and influential Anglo-Irish family, and grew up in Dublin. He was educated in Kilkenny, and then at Oxford and the Inns of Court; but he apparently converted to Catholicism in the late 1570s—he was a close friend of Edmund Campion's—and his position in Elizabethan England grew increasingly precarious. In 1579 he emigrated to the Netherlands, and remained on the continent for the rest of his life. He believed that the English spoken by the old Anglo-Irish was a purer form of the language than Elizabethan English, close to the English of Chaucer (it preserves, he says, "the dregs of the old Chaucer English"), without the modern mixture of continental tongues—this, of course, ignores the large French component of Chaucer's English. The diction of the Virgil translation, including its occasional egregious alliteration, was presumably designed as a version of the English he grew up with, an attempt to restore the old language—as Spenser was to characterize Chaucer as the "well of English undefiled."[14] Stanyhurst even characterizes the *Aeneid* as "a *Canterbury tale*," because, through impeccable language and versification, it "dooth labour, in telling . . . too ferret owt thee secretes of *Nature*." However farfetched the comparison, Chaucer is the benchmark.[15] This produced some startling effects. Here is Dido bewailing the fact that no child had been born of her love of Aeneas (the original spelling here is essential):

> . . . yf yeet soom progenye from me
> Had crawld, by the fatherd, yf a cockney-dandiprat hopthumb,
> Prittye lad Aeneas, in my court, wantoned, ere thow
> Took'st this filthye fleing, that thee with physnomye lyckned,
> I ne then had reckned my self for desolat ouwcaste. (sig. *L*3^{v})

Nashe was a capricious critic, to say the least, but he was in this case a literary barometer. Phaer and Twine's *Aeneid* was in no danger from Stanyhurst's, which was admired only by scholars; but the violent defense of the modern classic registers a real sense of panic. The sound of verse, the sense of what was good verse, the canons of taste, were all changing very rapidly. The change was part of a large cultural shift, from normative poets like William Higgins, John Heywood, and Gascoigne to normative poets like Jonson, Samuel Daniel, Michael Drayton, and especially Marlowe—think of Marlowe's contempt, at the same moment, for "jigging veins of rhyming motherwits" in the prologue to *Tamburlaine*. Marlowe is rejecting the prosody of popular drama such as *Cambises*, but that was also the prosody of Golding and Phaer. What Nashe deplores is the institution of a new "classical."

Stanyhurst, however, is not the culprit. Marlowe's sneer surely has an element of snobbery about it, the university graduate as arbiter of taste, of what constitutes high-class verse; declaring his own very popular drama to be nevertheless "classy"—or classic.

Barbaric Rhyme

For most critics, the really significant element in the reform of poetry was not an application of quantitative meters but the abandonment of rhyme. Rhyme was the crucial badge of barbarism, the essential departure from the classical ideal. Thus, Francis Meres, having compared Chaucer with Homer and declared him "the god of English poets," nevertheless singles out *Piers Plowman* as the one truly Homeric English poem: "As *Homer* was the first that adorned the Greek tongue with true quantity, so *Piers Plowman* was the first that observed the true quantitie of our verse without the curiositie of Rime."[16] That the poem is claimed to observe "true quantity" indicates how vague the sense of quantity in English could be. It is certainly arguable that Phaer's and Golding's fourteeners achieve a kind of prosodic "quantity," a supple and varied verse rhythm that is obviously not alien either to the English language or to the ballad measure within which they are working. The claim that the verse of *Piers Plowman* respects quantity is surely incorrect, but to Meres in 1598, the absence of rhyme was the key element.

For Campion in his *Observations in the arte of English poesie* (1602), it is fair to say that the absence of rhyme counted for almost everything. There is much that is quixotic about the treatise. To begin with, it is dedicated to Thomas Sackville, Lord Buckhurst, subsequently first Earl of Dorset, who in his youth had been the coauthor of *Gorboduc* and a principal contributor to *The Mirror for Magistrates*—that is, a notable poet of verse in both the newest and the most traditional styles, *Gorboduc* in blank verse, the *Mirror* poems in rhyme royal. By 1602 he had had an extensive political and diplomatic career, and was lord treasurer during the final years of Queen Elizabeth and the first years of King James. So far as is known, he had written no poetry for four decades, though *The Mirror for Magistrates* was still in print, and had the status of an English classic. Nevertheless, Campion announces to Sackville that he has "studyed to induce a true forme of versefying into our language: for the vulgar and unarteficiall custome of riming hath, I know, deter'd many excellent wits from the exercise of English poesy"[17]—it had not, of course, deterred Sackville from writing the heavily rhymed *Induction* and *Complaint of Henry Duke of Buckingham* in *The Mirror.* How seriously could he have taken a claim that rhyme royal was not a true form of versifying, and that its ubiquitous rhymes were vulgar, unartificial, and forbidding? Or did the blank verse of *Gorboduc* suggest to Campion that an argument against rhyme would find in Sackville a sympathetic ear? But probably all this is irrelevant; most likely Sackville was selected simply as a powerful aristocrat with an interest in, or at least a connection to, poetry; and the prestige conferred by his name at the start of the volume was all Campion expected from him.

Campion begins with what purports to be a historical argument:

> Learning first flourished in *Greece;* from thence it was derived unto the *Romaines,* both diligent observers of the number and quantity of sillables, not in their verses only but likewise in their prose. Learning, after the declining of the *Romaine* Empire and the pollution of their language through the conquest of the *Barbarians,* lay most pitifully deformed till the time of *Erasmus, Rewcline* [Reuchlin], Sir *Thomas More,* and other learned men of that age, who brought the Latine toong again to light, redeeming it with much labour out of the hands of the illiterate Monks and Friers. . . . In those lack-learning times, and in barbarized Italy, began that vulgar and easie kind of Poesie which is now in use throughout most parts of Christendome, which we abusively call Rime and Meeter.[18]

The claims here depend on a series of loaded terms and patently false assumptions—"the pollution of their language," "illiterate monks and friars"—and a rejection of "that vulgar and easie kind of Poesie which is now in use."

The arguments proposed against rhyme also depend on a series of unexamined assumptions:

> The eare is a rationall sence and a chiefe judge of proportion; but in our kind of riming what proportion is there kept where there remaines such a confused inequalitie of sillables? *Iambick* and *Trochaick* feete, which are opposed by nature, are by all Rimers confounded; nay, oftentimes they place instead of an *Iambick* the foot *Pyrrychius*, consisting of two short sillables, curtalling their verse, which they supply in reading with a ridiculous and vnapt drawing of their speech. As for example:
>
> Was it my desteny, or dismall chaunce?
>
> In this verse the two last sillables of the word *Desteny,* being both short, and standing for a whole foote in the verse, cause the line to fall out shorter then it ought by nature.[19]

"Shorter than it ought by nature": the appeal to nature is a refrain throughout the essay. Campion really seems to believe that the rules of classical prosody are not artificial but natural. As for the "ridiculous and unapt" pentameter example, it is to a modern ear felicitous enough, and must also have been in Campion's time, if "all rimers" confused iambs with trochees—"rimers" here must mean simply poets, since the conflation of metrical feet has nothing to do with rhyme.

But the clinching argument is presented as plain common sense: "If the *Italians*, *Frenchmen*, and *Spanyards*, that with commendation have written in Rime, were demaunded whether they had rather the bookes they haue publisht (if their toong would beare it) should remaine as they are in Rime or be translated into the auncient numbers of the Greekes and Romaines, would they not answere into numbers?"[20] The claim as it stands is preposterous. The question, however, could be reframed into one that any Renaissance poet would surely answer in the affirmative: would you like to be taken as seriously as Virgil or Homer—would you like to be a classical poet? Still, if the price were a translation into "ancient numbers," the vernacular poet might balk. There were certainly celebrated neo-Latin poets—Mantuan, Thomas More,

George Buchanan, Daniel Heinsius—but even in Campion's time the famous Petrarch poems were the sonnets, not the *Africa*, despite the fact that Petrarch's Latin epic was certainly channeling Virgil.

Campion's underlying claim, that there is more to English verse than stress and rhyme, is certainly valid; but classical metrics do not at all represent the rhythm of English. The extensive arguments in favor of the quantitative system are therefore accompanied, necessarily, by the invention of a set of rules for English quantity, though the animus is primarily directed against rhyme. It is surely to the point, however, that, aside from the examples given in the *Observations*, almost all Campion's own verse in English is rhymed, almost none of it is quantitative, and, despite the claims that the classical mode restores the essential relation of verse with music, he set only a single one of his own quantitative poems to music ("Come Let Us Sound with Melody"), leading one to wonder how feasible Campion himself considered his proposals to be. Indeed, Percival Vivian, editor of the Oxford edition of Campion's works, doubts that he even really understood the classical system, since for the most part Campion merely treats stressed syllables in English as long.[21] His difficulty with the long-by-position rule has already been noted.

The sole object of Samuel Daniel's rebuttal is, as the title indicates, *A Defence of Ryme* (1603). In fact, Daniel considers the quantitative system essentially an irrelevance: "We could well have allowed of his numbers had he not disgraced our Ryme; which both Custome and Nature doth most powerfully defend: Custome that is before all Law, Nature that is aboue all Arte." First, there is the nature of the language—the argument from nature here makes sense:

> Every language hath her proper number or measure fitted to use and delight, which, Custome intertaining by the allowance of the Eare, doth indenize, and make naturall. All verse is but a frame of wordes confinde within certaine measure; differing from the ordinarie speach, and introduced, the better to expresse mens conceipts, both for delight and memorie. Which frame of wordes consisting of *Rithmus* or *Metrum,* Number or measure, are disposed into divers fashions, according to the humour of the Composer and the set of the time. And these *Rhythmi* as *Aristotle* saith, are familiar amongst all Nations, and *è*

> *naturali & sponte fusa compositione* [natural and spontaneously flowing compositions]: and they fall as naturally already in our language as ever Art can make them, being such as the Eare of it selfe doth marshall in their proper roomes, and they of themselves will not willingly be put out of their ranke: and that in such a verse as best comports with the Nature of our language.

The justification of rhyme is simply that it gives pleasure: "And for our Ryme (which is an excellencie added to this worke of measure, and a Harmonie, farre happier than any proportion Antiquitie could euer shew us) dooth adde more grace, and hath more of delight than ever bare numbers, howsoever they can be forced to runne in our slow language, can possibly yeeld."[22] There is a commonsense argument here, to which Campion could not have given the easy reply that he himself takes no delight in rhyme, since so much of his own poetry is rhymed. To the claim that classical prosody when applied to "our slow language" is "forced," however, the reply would have to be that all poetry is "forced," in the sense that it is composed according to some system. The stumbling block is the system: to compose English poetry in classical metrics, it is necessary either to misrepresent or remake the language. The language is misrepresented when the second syllable of Trumpington is claimed to be "naturally" long; the language is remade when "by" is spelled "bi," to pretend that the syllable has thereby become short.

Daniel's treatise was on the right side of history, but his arguments are no more rational than Campion's: both depend on assumptions of consensus about what is natural to the language and gives pleasure in verse. The practice of English prosody by Campion's and Daniel's time was not rule-bound; and indeed, George Gascoigne, in his *Certayne Notes of Instruction Concerning the Making of Verse or Ryme in English* (1575) observes that the most elementary precept, that a metrical system established at the poem's outset ought to be observed throughout, is ignored in "many mens poems now adayes," not as an expression of freedom and inventiveness, but merely through "forgetfulnes or carelesnes."[23] So the maker of systems despairs at the outset. George Puttenham's *Arte of English Poesie* (1589) is far more compendious, but it is a survey of the vast variety of current practice rather than a rule book; and even

Sidney's only stipulations for poets in his *Apologie* are to teach and delight and imitate the ancients—the last of these is the difficult part, and we inevitably fail. Indeed, if the classical rules were ever codified in ancient times, neither that treatise nor any reference to it has survived. What we know as classical prosody was systematized much later, deduced from a study of classical practice; and if the rules are correct, even the ancients sometimes did not follow them.[24]

Chapter 4

What Classical Looks Like

The Return of the Repressed

If the poetic examples give us some sense of what the classical sounded like in Tudor and Stuart England, what did the classical look like? To us, the classical looks like the Venus de Milo or the Apollo Belvedere—these are ancient statues, but the idea of the classical they embody is the one that Michelangelo's Renaissance authorized, which only reached England two centuries later in the era of William Kent and Robert Adam, subsequently filtered through the aesthetic theories of Winckelmann and enshrined in the Elgin Marbles: white, pure, thoroughly idealized. But even the Elgin Marbles, if you look closely, give the show away: they have traces of pigment on them. In their original state, they were painted to look lifelike.

Recent reconstructions of ancient sculpture restoring their coloring, however, show them looking more like waxworks than like either life or art.[1] Most of us would agree that such reconstructions look dreadful—from our standpoint, the ancients paid a heavy price for authenticity. And though the Italians must have known that the statues they were digging up had the remains of pigment on them, nobody ever proposed painting the David to look lifelike—the rebirth of the classical was always revisionary. Still, the pediments of the Philadelphia Art Museum, completed in 1928, have their figures in full color, an attempt at how the Parthenon really looked.[2] The gods are a little stiff—Philadelphia had no Phidias—but from afar, the groups are dignified and convincing enough. This is certainly classical in spirit; it suggests to us, however, not ancient Greece but a much less animated version of Raphael's frescoes of the gods in the Farnesina in Rome, or Giulio Romano's mythological narratives in the Palazzo Tè in Mantua—that is, not at all classical, entirely of the Renaissance.

One could say, however, that Raphael's and Giulio's vibrant colors constitute the return of the repressed—everything about the past that the "rebirth" of the classical omitted. The sixteenth and seventeenth centuries' classical was, in addition, far more capacious than the graceful and heroic pantheon of the Italian Renaissance. The greatest collection of classical remains in Stuart England was the Arundel Marbles. The earl and countess had travelled to Italy in 1613 and 1614, taking with them as their guide and artistic adviser Inigo Jones, already established as a designer and architect. Over three decades, the Arundels formed a magnificent art collection, including both ancient and modern works, and commissioned Daniel Mytens to do portraits of themselves before their treasures (Figures 2 and 3). Their collection, however, was really not what we would call an art gallery. The Arundel Marbles seem to us the forerunners of the Elgin Marbles; but they looked quite different to contemporary observers.

Arundel's protégé Henry Peacham in *The Compleat Gentleman* (1634) praises the statues in terms that are indicative: there is nothing about ideal Greek bodies or perfect proportion or contrapposto, and not really much about aesthetics. The sculptures bring the past to life; they give the observer, he says, "the pleasure of seeing, and conversing with these old *Heroes*." Moreover, and perhaps most significantly, as we shall see, "the profit of knowing them, redounds to all Poets, Painters, Architects, and generally to such as may have occasion to imploy any of these, and by consequent, to all Gentlemen." As for Arundel House, Peacham calls it "the chief English scene of ancient Inscriptions. . . . You shall finde all the walles of the house inlayde with them, and speaking Greeke and Latine to you. The Garden especially will affoord you the pleasure of a world of learned Lectures in this kinde."[3] Thus John Selden's book entitled *Marmora Arundelliana* (1629) includes not only depictions of sculptures but also many pages like the one in Figure 4, epitomes of "a world of learned lectures." The classical languages have become

Figure 2. Daniel Mytens, *Alathea Howard Countess of Arundel* before the gallery. ©*National Portrait Gallery, London.*

an aristocratic touchstone, and the collecting passion was not simply aesthetic. It also involved a profound interest in recovering and preserving the past, an education in both history and sensibility. Most strikingly, classical connoisseurship has become the badge of a gentleman, who is here identified with the artist, marked as much by his taste as by his lineage.

Figure 3. Daniel Mytens, *Thomas Howard Earl of Arundel* before the gallery. ©*National Portrait Gallery, London.*

Such a claim involves quite a new notion of both gentleman and artist. In 1629, the year in which Selden published *Marmora Arundelliana*, Peter Paul Rubens wrote from London to a friend in Paris of "the incredible quantity of excellent pictures, statues, and ancient inscriptions which are to be found in this Court"—the inscriptions are mentioned in the same breath as the

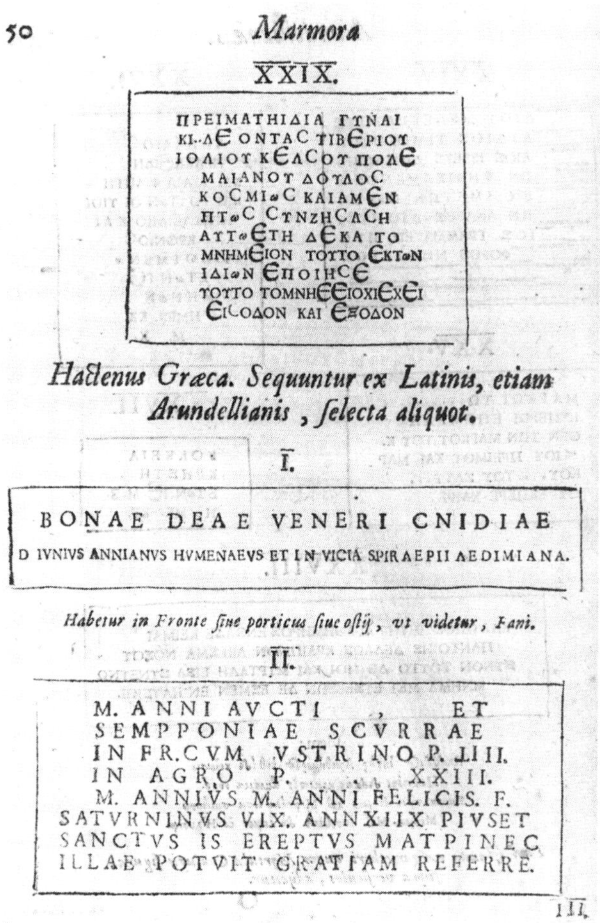
50 *Marmora*

XXIX.

ΠΡΕΙΜΑΤΗΙΔΙΑ ΓΥΝΑΙ
ΚΙ..ΔΕ ΟΝΤΑC ΤΙΒΕΡΙΟΥ
ΙΟΛΙΟΥ ΚΕΛCΟΥ ΠΟΛΕ
ΜΑΙΑΝΟΥ ΔΟΥΛΟC
ΚΟCΜΙωC ΚΑΙΑΜΕΝ
ΠΤωC CΥΝΖΗCΑCΗ
ΑΥΤωΕΤΗ ΔΕΚΑ ΤΟ
ΜΝΗΜΕΙΟΝ ΤΟΥΤΟ ΕΚΤωΝ
ΙΔΙωΝ ΕΠΟΙΗCΕ
ΤΟΥΤΟ ΤΟΜΝΗΕΕΙΟΧΙΕΧΕΙ
ΕΙCΟΔΟΝ ΚΑΙ ΕΞΟΔΟΝ

Hactenus Græca. Sequuntur ex Latinis, etiam Arundellianis, ſelecta aliquot.

I.

BONAE DEAE VENERI CNIDIAE
D IVNIVS ANNIANVS HVMENAEVS ET IN VICIA SPIRAEPII AEDIMIANA.

Habetur in Fronte ſiue porticus ſiue oſtij, vt videtur, Fani.

II.

M. ANNI AVCTI , ET
SEMPPONIAE SCVRRAE
IN FR.CVM VSTRINO P. LIII.
IN AGRO P. XXIII.
M. ANNIVS M. ANNI FELICIS. F.
SATVRNINVS VIX. ANNXIIX PIVSET
SANCTVS IS EREPTVS MATPINEC
ILLAE POTVIT GRATIAM REFERRE.

III.

Figure 4. Inscriptions from John Selden, *Marmora Arundelliana*, 1629.

works of art. His highest praise was reserved for one of Arundel's sculptures: "I confess that I have never seen anything in the world more rare, from the point of view of antiquity."[4] As the last bit suggests, to collectors like Arundel and artists like Rubens, a primary value of the visual and plastic arts was their memorializing quality, their link to the past and the vision of permanence they implied. This is why Peacham emphasizes the importance and rarity not only of the statues but of the inscriptions: they were an essential element of the artistic power of the past. The word established the significance, the authority, of classical imagery; and modern masterpieces, the work of Giambologna, Michelangelo, Rubens, existed in a direct continuum with the arts of Greece and Rome. They would not have seemed so to our eyes: many of the figural works are stiff votive images or tomb effigies, portraits of often elderly or middle-aged people, thoroughly clothed and not at all "classically" beautiful.[5] For us, these are archeology, not art. But to an England in search of the classical world, they were a real link with the life of the past, especially through its death.

Mythography

Moreover, the mythographers and iconographers admitted into the classical pantheon a host of hybrid figures who appear to us not at all classical, but merely grotesque. Vincenzo Cartari's *Le imagini de i dei de gli antichi*, a standard handbook for artists published in many editions from 1556 on well into the seventeenth century, includes many images like that in Figure 5, of a hawk-headed Apollo as the Sun with a three-headed Hecate as the moon (the heads are a dog, a boar, and a horse). And in fact, classical religion was far more strange and multifarious than classical poetry acknowledged, and was never defined by the fixed pantheon found in literary texts, to say nothing of purified mythology after Winckelmann, the mythology of Bullfinch and Robert Graves. The Olympian gods in Virgil and Ovid are essentially engaged in domestic comedy; but even for Ovid, the divine is a history of animal transformations—Jove as a bull, a swan, an eagle—and the Apollo myth begins with the hero's defeat of a gigantic serpent, a divine python, the remnant of an earlier cult which remained incorporated into the worship of this most rational of the gods. This is the classical that Roberto Calasso describes in *Le nozze di Cadmo e Armonia*, frightening, monstrous.[6] In late antiquity the Roman cults also imported the Egyptian gods, the dog-headed Anubis, the hawk-headed Horus and Ra, the ram-headed Khnum. The Renaissance felt no need to purge these as alien or inappropriate: the ancient gods to the sixteenth century constituted an endlessly malleable symbolic repertory. The classical was a mode of expression enabled by a pantheon of meaning.

Figure 5. Bolognino Zaltieri, Apollo as the sun, Hecate as the moon, illustration in Vincenzo Cartari, *Le imagini de i dei de gli antichi*, 1571.

The meaning, moreover, could be infinitely adjustable. Thus, Lilio Gregorio Giraldi, the most scholarly of the sixteenth-century mythographers, explains the figure of Saturn as variously a legendary king of Italy, a personification of heaven or of time, and a fertility figure—he sees no need to choose among these interpretations. Natalis Comes (Natale Conti, Noël le Comte), the most broadly influential of the mythographers after Boccaccio's pioneering *Genealogiae Deorum*, sees contradictions as of the essence in the ancient stories, not to be adjudicated or resolved. Here is a widely discussed example. The marriage of Vulcan with any of a number of beautiful goddesses (variously Venus, Minerva, or one of the Graces) is often read as a transparent allegory: the alliance of beauty with craftsmanship produces the art exemplified in Achilles's shield. This is elegantly simple, but appears to us also simplistic, not least because it ignores the fact that the marriage was notoriously unhappy. The allegory is suspect precisely in its simplicity: we have learned from Lévi-Strauss that myths are not so easily accounted for. Modern commentators therefore declare this a late rationalization, and reject it as an explanation of the story. Renaissance mythography, however, has scarcely begun. Cartari and others go on to explain that the beautiful goddess and the ugly smith were married because nothing can be created without warmth: Venus signifies creativity or generation; and Vulcan, as god of fire, signifies heat. This is, for us, even more farfetched. But, the commentators continue, in those versions of the story in which Vulcan is denied Minerva's hand in marriage, he fails to win her because craftsmanship is not invariably successful in executing what invention conceives. As an interpretation, this appears to the modern mind simply a desperate rationalization. Several Renaissance accounts, however, give it pride of place. There are in addition any number of more specialized moralizations, natural, astronomical, alchemical (the last is the only one scoffed at by Comes), and so forth. The characteristic quality of these moralizations is that they leave the story intact, and nothing in them precludes any number of alternative and even contradictory interpretations. Comes, in fact, remains one of the most genuinely useful of the mythographers, precisely because he sees contradictions as of the essence, and does not try to resolve them—for Comes (as several centuries later for Lévi-Strauss) mythology is an expression of the irresolvable contradictions in the culture.

These handbooks were tremendously influential throughout the European Renaissance, informing poetry, philosophy, and the arts generally. Nevertheless, there were no English editions of any of the mythographers, and hardly any translations—mythography was clearly felt by the English to be dangerously close to false religion. Stephen Batman's survey *The Golden Booke of the Leaden Goddes* (1577) is indicative: it includes among its pagan deities a number of heretics and Anabaptists. The classical pantheon here constituted, as the title page announces, "the vayne imaginations of Heathen Pagans, and counterfaict Christians"—the only surprise, since Batman was an Anglican clergyman, is that no popes or Roman Catholic theologians are included. A translation of Cartari by Richard Linche appeared in 1599 under the title *The Fountaine of Ancient Fiction*—since the *Imagini* was an iconology, not a mythography, there was less to be nervous about, and the translation was clearly responding to the growing English market for the visual arts. Francis Bacon's mythographic essay *De Sapientia Veterum* (The Wisdom of the Ancients) avoids issues of faith entirely, making the pagan myths allegories of science, not religion. And though such Elizabethan and Jacobean writers as Spenser and Jonson were thoroughly familiar with the standard continental mythographic source books, a substantial version of Comes's essential mythography first appears in English only in the commentary included by George Sandys in the second edition of his translation of Ovid's *Metamorphoses*, published in 1632.

Imagining the Classical

The classical, as the mythographers expounded it, was a rich and complex mixture, including much that was grotesque, mysterious, and dark; and of course classical literature offered models for tragedy and satire, as well as for praise and celebration. The classical in architecture was seemingly another matter, supremely rational, mathematically proportioned and governed by rules, admitting the grotesque only as grace notes, a kind of punctuation—by the middle of the sixteenth century in England, to classicize architecturally in the modern Italian and French style was a mode of idealization. Nevertheless, the complex mixture is often still evident.

The astonishing mannerist portrait of the Earl of Surrey at the age of 29 (see the Frontispiece), is ascribed to the Netherlandish painter William Scrots, though it is said by the National Portrait Gallery, which now owns it, to be the work of an unknown Italian artist—the vagueness reflects how very uncharacteristic the painting is (the consensus is that it is a Jacobean copy of a Scrots painting). It is dated 1546, the year before Surrey's execution for treason, and shows him elongated at full length, dressed in fantastic finery, posed within an arch and leaning on a broken column. He is surrounded by both classical sculptures and the royal emblems that were to be cited at his trial as evidence of his treasonable intentions. The mannerist-classical context was, of course, a continental import—as, for the most part, all art was—but it is an index to the developing aesthetic style of the age, to how Britons of taste and position wanted to see and present themselves.

Too little is known about Scrots, if the artist is he, to say what he might have been looking at, but the obvious analogues are mannerist portraits by Bronzino and Pontormo and Fontainebleau paintings and prints. Morten Steen Hansen has identified the source of the figures and masks around the arch as an anonymous Fontainbleau etching of the 1540s (Figure 6): the copy is very precise.[7] Artists working in England in the mid-sixteenth century had a repertory of classical imagery close at hand. They would also have been familiar with the work of Hans Holbein, who preceded Scrots as painter to the English court (and was paid less than half Scrots's salary). But there really are no obvious models for the way this image is classicized. Bronzino portraits of connoisseurs and artists typically include a few architectural details and an occasional small sculpture. Holbein's 1520 portrait of the quintessential classicist Erasmus is posed next to a single ionic pilaster, and holds a book titled in Greek *The Labors of Hercules*; his portrait of Surrey, done around 1540, is restrained and unadorned, a simple bust—Surrey at 23, wrapped in a plain dark cloak, is withdrawn and dour, not at all the showman of Scrots's painting. Scrots's other portraits, for example of Edward VI as prince and king, show the same richly detailed clothing, but nothing like the elaboration of the symbolic surroundings; hence, presumably, the Portrait Gallery's change in the attribution. But the assertiveness of the classical framing here was surely part of the commission (as the inclusion of the shields with their presumptuous heraldry must have been), a true expression of the client's sense of himself as he reached his mature years.[8]

Fifty years later, by the turn of the century, the England of Marlowe, Shakespeare, Jonson was imbued with the classics, not only in literature, but

Figure 6. School of Fontainbleau etching, ca. 1542–1545 (compare the frontispiece). Metropolitan Museum of Art, New York.

visually, as aristocrats began adding colonnades to their houses (not always very effectively, as in the lumpish example at Hardwick Hall in Figure 7, built in the 1590s for the formidable Bess of Shrewsbury), and churches began to look like Roman temples; Figure 8 is Wenceslaus Hollar's view of St. Paul's Covent Garden, designed by Inigo Jones in 1631. Jones also declared the Neolithic Stonehenge to be the remains of a Roman shrine (thus updating it by a couple of thousand years), and imagined it as a classical monument (Figure 9), though far more austerely classical than anything authentically Roman—classicism was always revisionary.

Books adopted the typography of ancient Roman inscriptions for their dedications, as in the famous example in Figure 10, and by the 1590s printers were switching from black letter to roman type. This was medieval Italian, not ancient Roman,[9] but it represented a decisive move away from the traditional

Figure 7. Hardwick Hall, Derbyshire.

Figure 8. Wenceslaus Hollar, *The Piazza in Covent Garden*, ca. 1644. Davison Art Center, Wesleyan University.

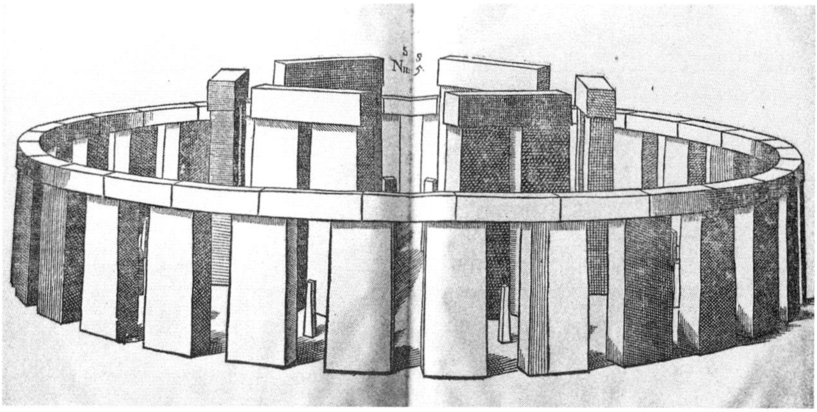

Figure 9. After Inigo Jones, reconstruction of Stonehenge. From Inigo Jones, *The Most Notable Antiquity of Great Britain, vulgarly called Stone-Heng*, London, 1655.

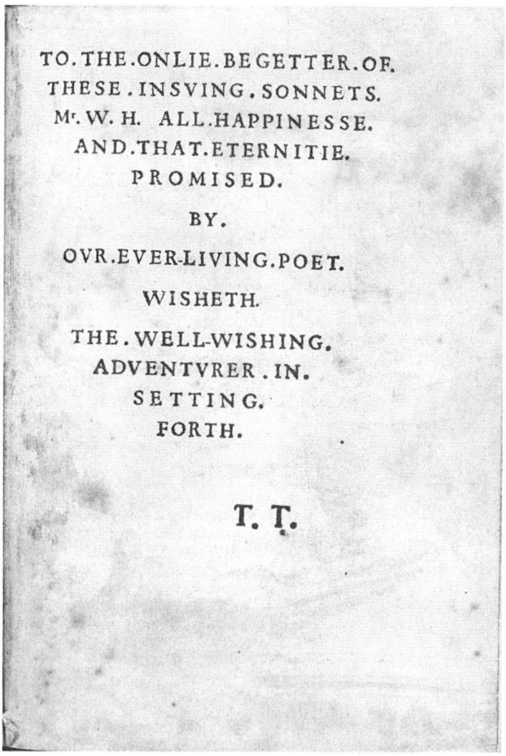

TO.THE.ONLIE.BEGETTER.OF.
THESE.INSVING.SONNETS.
Mr.W. H. ALL.HAPPINESSE.
AND.THAT.ETERNITIE.
PROMISED.
BY.
OVR.EVER-LIVING.POET.
WISHETH.
THE.WELL-WISHING.
ADVENTVRER.IN.
SETTING.
FORTH.

T. T.

Figure 10. Shake-speares Sonnets, 1609, Dedication. Folger Shakespeare Library.

English look, and it was a classicizing move in the sense that roman had been the typography for Latin texts published in England from the first decade of the century. For printers, the typographic transformation was a hugely expensive business, involving the acquisition of whole new sets of fonts, which gives a sense of how powerful the change in taste was.

The Talismanic Arts

The arts, indeed, took on an iconic, even talismanic, quality in the period, with classicism at its center. Near the end of *The Winter's Tale* we are told of a surpassingly lifelike statue of the late queen Hermione, the work of "that rare Italian master Giulio Romano," commissioned and owned by the noble Paulina, connoisseur and architect of the play's reconciliations. In the final scene, the statue is revealed, and brought to life. The invocation of Giulio Romano is striking for a number of reasons: this is the only allusion in Shakespeare to a modern artist and, indeed, one of the earliest references to Giulio in England—Shakespeare here, as nowhere else, appears to be in touch with the avant-garde of the visual arts. But Giulio was not a sculptor, and in fact the name is all the play gives us—as it turns out, there is no statue; the figure Paulina unveils is the living queen.

The relation between art and life is particularly direct here, and the ability of the great artist to restore the losses of the past and reconcile the present to them is represented as axiomatic. But the name of the artist is essential, the name of an artist renowned for his skill at producing the illusion of life; and a modern artist, moreover, not a historical figure like Phidias or Zeuxis, who might be expected to be supplying art treasures in ancient Sicily, where *The Winter's Tale* is set. Paulina is presented in the play as a connoisseur, the owner of a collection of artistic rarities; she knows what she is doing, and her expertise reminds us that the collecting instinct was starting to burgeon in the England of 1610—we return to the Earl and Countess of Arundel presiding over the greatest collection of art works in Jacobean England. They owned, indeed, a number of Giulio's drawings, including preparatory sketches for the luxuriantly lifelike frescoes at the Palazzo Tè, though these had not been acquired by 1610.

Still, the Arundel circle would have been a good source of information about what artists were both in vogue and especially adept at the lifelike.

There was, in fact, a good deal of information circulating in Shakespeare's England about who were the right artists to invest in. Richard Haydocke, translator of an artistic handbook by Paolo Lomazzo published in English in 1598, noted "some of our Nobility, and divers private Gentlemen, have . . . their Galleries carefully furnished, with the excellent monuments of sundry famous ancient masters, both Italian and Germane,"[10] and English collectors in the first decade of the seventeenth century began for the first time to be serious connoisseurs, dispatching experts to the continent to buy for them, and concerned with acquiring expertise of their own. In 1609, the Earl of Exeter was advising the Earl of Shrewsbury to purchase paintings by Palma Giovane and sculpture by Giambologna, suggestions both shrewd and in the best modern taste.[11] Prince Henry became a passionate collector of paintings and bronzes. By 1610 Inigo Jones's expertise was being employed: he had travelled in Italy by this time, and was advising first the Earl of Rutland on artistic matters, and later the Prince of Wales and the Arundels.

On the continent conspicuous collections of great art had for more than a century been an attribute of princely magnificence. Henry VIII had to some extent undertaken to emulate his contemporaries Francis I and Charles V in this respect: there were no Titians in the Tudor royal gallery, but the Holbeins and Torrigianos suggest a very high standard of artistic taste (the king, however, spent lavishly on tapestries, and only modestly on paintings). The royal taste was obviously not genetic: Queen Mary's court painter was Antonio Mor, not a bad choice, but hardly in the league of Holbein; and neither Elizabeth nor James had much interest in the arts as such, nor had they any interest whatever in spending money to increase the royal collection. But King James nevertheless provides a directly topical source for Paulina's statue: in 1605 he commissioned sculptures of Queen Elizabeth and of his mother, Mary Queen of Scots, who had been executed for treason against Elizabeth in 1587. These were effigies for their monuments in Westminster Abbey—James's treasonous mother was to be rehabilitated by being reburied among the kings and queens of England. Elizabeth's statue was completed in 1607, Mary's before 1612; both statues were lifelike, in the sense that they were painted, as Hermione's is said to be, and as effigies always were in the period. The royal patron of Shakespeare's company was not a connoisseur or a collector, but he nevertheless relied on the power of art to memorialize, reconcile, and restore.

Let us begin with his son Prince Henry's collection. He seems to have been introduced to connoisseurship around 1610, when he was sixteen, by Robert Cecil, Earl of Salisbury, and Arundel. Cecil already had a notable collection (he was furnishing Hatfield House), including mythological and biblical subjects by both Italian and Netherlandish artists. At Henry's request he sent a group of paintings for the prince's attention; it went without saying that one of them would remain with the prince as a gift to form the nucleus of a royal collection that would stamp this prince as a true Renaissance monarch. Cecil was to accompany the pictures and expound their merits (and presumably to ensure that Henry chose the right one to keep with the Earl's compliments). He was advised, however, that if he was unable to come himself, "you may send my lord of Arundel as deputy to set forth the praise of your pictures"—Arundel was the real expert.[12]

The painting Cecil gave the prince was Palma Giovane's *Prometheus Chained to the Caucasus* (Figure 11).[13] It had been acquired for him in 1608 by Sir Henry Wotton, the English ambassador in Venice. It is still in the royal collection, though it is not much regarded now, and it *is* rather grim. Nevertheless, it really can be considered one of the foundational works of English artistic taste, a touchstone that almost by itself established the market for Venetian painting in England. Wotton, indeed, had sent it to Cecil in the first place in order to establish his own credentials as an artistic agent and broker. There were, to be sure, some Venetian paintings in English collections already—the Earl of Leicester is said to have owned some, though no catalogue of them has survived, and Leicester's nephew Sir Philip Sidney, always in the avant-garde of taste, knew enough to sit for his portrait by Veronese when he was in Venice (this was initially not a success; Hubert Languet, to whom Sidney sent it, was disappointed in it, complaining that it made him look too young, and it has since disappeared). But Palma's *Prometheus* was the work that made everyone want big dramatic Venetian paintings, not just Palmas, but the bigger (and more expensive) names: Titians, Tintorettos, Veroneses. Thereafter it was made clear that gentlemen desiring Prince Henry's favor could do no better than give him paintings.

Figure 11. Palma Giovane, *Prometheus Chained to the Caucasus* (also called *Tityus Chained to the Rock*). Royal Collection Trust / © Her Majesty Queen Elizabeth II 2020.

The prince's own taste, insofar as one can judge it, was eclectic, voracious, and relatively uninformed. The largest purchases were Dutch and Flemish, but that was only because the market was closer and the agents more familiar: he was in fact the first large purchaser of Venetian paintings in England. When he asks for gifts from continental princes eager to curry favor with the next king of England, the requests are little short of megalomaniac: not merely miniature bronzes by Giambologna (in response he received a number of miniature *copies* of Giambologna statues) but the famous life-size *Rape of the Sabines* in the Piazza Signoria in Florence, and a Michelangelo ceiling from the Palazzo Medici in Siena. (This last—both the ceiling and the palace—fortunately did not exist, so a refusal was easy.) But the collection was to consist not only of works by famous artists; the subject matter was as important as the artist, and in some cases more important. Henry asked for and was sent portraits of illustrious men, such as had graced the royal gallery of Cosimo de' Medici—being a Renaissance prince meant imitating the lifestyles of the rich and famous. Hence there were also scenes of important battles on land and sea, night pieces, exercises in perspective and *trompe l'oeil* combining art with the new science of optics; even scientific instruments were included. There was a model of a perpetual motion machine constructed by the prince's resident magus Cornelius Drebbel (this worked by changes in barometric pressure, and was somehow supposed to demonstrate the validity of the Ptolemaic system against the claims of Copernicus and Galileo). Indeed, the request for the miniatures and the Michelangelo ceiling was accompanied by further requests for a new type of magnet and the latest book by Galileo (was the prince unpersuaded by Drebbel's machine?), as well as for the plans of Michelangelo's staircase in the Laurentian library in Florence, and the formula for a new cement capable of sealing pipes so they could carry water uphill without leaking. The art gallery was also to be a historical and scientific museum, a cabinet of wonders, perhaps most of all an architectural masterpiece including elaborate fountains and waterworks.[14]

The Arundel collection was less eclectic than Prince Henry's, but once again, it was not merely a reflection of the new connoisseurship. Here is a very clear example of the age's assumptions about the function and power of art. The earl and countess conceived their collection not only as a private matter, treasures for their personal enjoyment, but as an education in taste for the nation—as such, it would also serve, of course, as a monument to their own taste and magnificence. To this end Arundel commissioned Wenceslaus Hollar to produce etchings of the principal masterpieces, with a view to publishing a volume of them.

One of the first that Hollar completed was a rather grisly scene from ancient history, *King Seleucis Ordering His Son's Eye to Be Put Out,* after a sketch by Giulio Romano for a fresco in the Palazzo Tè (Figure 12). The subject was a moral story about the perquisites and obligations of power: the son had committed adultery, the stipulated punishment for which was that the perpetrator's

Figure 12. Wenceslaus Hollar, after Giulio Romano, *King Seleucis Ordering His Son's Eye to Be Put Out* (also called *Zaleucus and His Son*), 1637. Metropolitan Museum of Art, New York.

eyes were to be put out. The father, as king, could have repealed the sentence, but instead he chose merely to mitigate it by ordering that only one of his son's eyes be blinded. The etching could certainly have stood on its own, a record of an exemplary work by one of the greatest Renaissance history painters, but it comes accompanied with a set of inscriptions. First Henry Peacham moralizes the scene in a Latin epigram which effectively suppresses the fact that the story is as much an instance of judicial nepotism as of justice tempered with mercy—one always had to be told how to take historical examples, which have an uncomfortable tendency to imply the wrong morals along with the right ones. Below this Hollar places a dedication to Arundel establishing all his credentials: his hereditary titles, his position as earl marshal, his Garter knighthood, and the assertion that he is the greatest amateur, collector, and promoter of the visual arts in the world. Hollar then establishes his own claims to artistic eminence: "This picture, first drawn by Giulio Romano"—notice how long it takes to get to the artist—"now preserved in Arundel House, and here engraved after the original, Wenceslaus Hollar humbly dedicates and consecrates," and so forth. The drawing comes accompanied with both a pedigree and an ethical commentary, a "learned lecture"; these are both essential to the picture.

Arundel's paintings served him as a species of validation, establishing not only his taste but his authority within his own history as well. Early in his career he began collecting Holbein portraits, of which a number had come to him by inheritance. Holbeins were very expensive in England at this time, as much for nationalistic reasons (the artist's record of Henry VIII and his court) as for his artistic excellence. But he had a particular connection with the Arundels, having painted many of the earl's ancestors, including the unfortunate Henry Howard, Earl of Surrey, who had been executed for treason; so the expense was also undertaken to assemble a visible family history. It undeniably helped to establish the earl's fame as a connoisseur—Arundel House contained over thirty Holbein oil portraits—but here again, the history was as important as the aesthetics, as the following story shows. In 1620 Cosimo de' Medici II, the Grand Duke of Tuscany, wrote requesting one of the earl's Holbeins as a gift; he offered to send any of his own paintings in exchange. He was, he wrote, "passionately set upon having a work by this artist."[15] Arundel dispatched a splendid portrait of Sir Richard Southwell, duly furnished with appropriate inscriptions praising the artist, memorializing the sitter, and identifying the donor and recipient connoisseurs by their coats of arms—once again, the inscriptions were considered essential to the work of art.

Now for Arundel, the Southwell portrait was a piece of family history in the worst way: Southwell had been instrumental in the arrest and execution of the Earl of Surrey. If the decision to purge the art collection of an old enemy seems logical, however, this in fact was not Arundel's motive. He at once commissioned a copy of the painting, and it continued to hang among the ancestors Southwell had betrayed. However demonic the sitter, whatever else the painting was, it was history. For Cosimo, on the other hand, it was both art and a testimony to his authority as a collector, and he hung it among the greatest treasures of the Uffizi, in the Tribuna, where it was still to be seen when Johann Zoffany visited Florence in 1777 and recorded its presence there.

After Prince Henry's death in 1612, Prince Charles inherited most of his brother's treasures, and, with the advice and encouragement of two of his father's favorites, Somerset and Buckingham (Charles and Arundel were on the whole not on good terms), added constantly to them, both by purchasing other collections and by commissioning paintings from the major artists of the day, most significantly Rubens and van Dyck. By the mid-1630s the Caroline royal pictures constituted one of the greatest art collections in the world. There was more in this acquisitive passion than aesthetics and conspicuous consumption. Just as in the sixteenth century artists came increasingly to be considered not mere craftsmen but philosophers and sages (thus the greatest artist of the age is referred to, in the account of his funeral, as "the divine Michelangelo"), so increasingly in the period great art was felt, in a way that was at once pragmatic and quasi-mystical, to be a manifestation of the power and authority of its possessor. Great artists became essential to the developing concept of monarchy and to the idealization of the increasingly watered-down aristocracy, to realize and deploy the imagery of legitimacy and greatness, providing, for example, in van Dyck's famous 1640 equestrian portrait of Charles I, an imperial persona for the beleaguered king on the eve of the Civil War.

The extent to which the power of art became a practical reality in England at this time may be gauged by a brief comparison of two large royal expenditures. In 1627, in the midst of the long and disastrous war England waged with Spain and subsequently with France, the Duke of Buckingham led an expedition to relieve a trapped Huguenot garrison at La Rochelle. But his troops proved insufficient, and in urgent need of reinforcements and pay for the soldiers, he appealed to the king. Charles believed wholeheartedly in the cause, but money was difficult to find; after three weeks, £14,000 and 2,000 additional troops were committed to the enterprise. These proved utterly inadequate, and Buckingham was forced to retreat ignominiously. Throughout this period, however, Charles was eagerly negotiating for the magnificent art collection of the Gonzaga Dukes of Mantua, which had recently come on the market, including Mantegna's vast *Triumph of Caesar*, still one of the glories of the British royal collection. For this Charles paid, in 1627 and 1628, a total of £25,500.[16] To this monarch, a royal gallery was worth far more than a successful army.

I turn now to the uses of art to power in this period. I have suggested its function as a way of memorializing and restoring, and the way it serves as a link with the past, something that brings to the present the authority and significance of history. But as van Dyck's heroic image of the shy and intellectual Charles I suggests, it functions also as a way of remaking the present. Daniel Mytens's portraits of Arundel and his countess before their gallery express the authority of this aristocratic couple specifically through both their taste and their ability to afford the vast expenditures necessary to acquire such treasures. In these images the sitters epitomize the concept of magnificence, what Aristotle defined as the virtue of princes, and though there is obviously a good deal of idealization at work here, the collection and the taste were real.

Figure 13, in contrast, is Rubens's version of the earl in a military persona: the connoisseur is replaced by the active hero. The only property visible here is his armor, but the classical triumphal arch before which he poses provides the necessary idealization. Unlike the portraits with the art collection, however, this one is pure fantasy: by 1629, when the picture was painted, Arundel had had no military experience whatever. He held his first military office only ten years later, when the king appointed him general of the army against the Scots, a position in which he served for all of three months, at which time the unsuccessful army was disbanded. Clarendon said of him that he had "nothing martial about him but his presence and his looks," and that he was made a general for "his negative qualities: he did not love the Scots, he did not love the Puritans."[17] The artist is supplying what life had denied him; but this was also both a way that Arundel wanted to be seen and a way he needed to see himself, not simply as a connoisseur, bureaucrat, aristocrat, but as a man of action in the line of descent from his heroic ancestors.

Any collection is the expression of the collector's taste and personality, in the fullest sense a manifestation of his—and in the case of the Arundels, her—mind. And as my examples have already indicated, the most enlightening part of any collection in the period is not what is bought but what is commissioned: the crucial pictures in Renaissance collections are the portraits of the patrons, those specific manifestations of their view of themselves (it is to the point that Veronese did not see Sidney as Sidney's admirers wanted him to be seen; it is probably also to the point that the painting does not survive). Let us return to Prince Henry and look at an aristocratic image in the process of creation.

Figure 13. Peter Paul Rubens, *Thomas Howard Earl of Arundel,* 1629–1630. Isabella Stewart Gardner Museum, Boston.

Prince Henry is an ideal case, because the iconographic documentation is so thorough and the time span so brief. Henry was born in 1594. He became Prince of Wales (and was thus formally declared the heir to the throne) in 1610, at the age of sixteen, and died two years later, probably of typhoid fever. He embodied, for that brief two years, all the militant idealism of Protestant England chafing under a pacifist king who was increasingly pro-Catholic. All the portraits we shall consider were done during that two-year period.

Figure 14 is the standard official portrait, by Robert Peake; Henry is aged about sixteen. The picture can be dated by the ostrich feathers on his hat: these are the emblem of the Prince of Wales, hence the date must be after his investiture in 1610. He is presented as a slim, boyish, serious, splendidly appointed young man; the idealization is all in the clothing, the properties, the decor—the white satin doublet lavishly embroidered with gold and jewels, the jeweled

Figure 14. Robert Peake, *Henry Frederick Prince of Wales*, ca. 1610, Investiture portrait. © National Portrait Gallery, London.

pompoms on the shoes, the Order of the Garter on his left leg, the Saint George medal around his neck, the gold-handled sword, the jeweled hat, the rich oriental rug on which he stands, his parklands beyond the window. Figure 15, painted during the next year, is an Isaac Oliver portrait miniature; the boyishness is gone, and the figure has been significantly classicized: this is basically the cameo portrait of a Roman emperor. Figure 16 is another Isaac Oliver portrait of 1611.

Figure 15. Isaac Oliver, *Henry Frederick Prince of Wales*, ca. 1611. ©*National Portrait Gallery, London.*

Figure 16. Isaac Oliver, *Henry Frederick Prince of Wales*, 1611. Royal Collection Trust / © Her Majesty Queen Elizabeth II 2020.

Figure 17. Prince Henry, frontispiece to Michael Drayton, *Poly-Olbion*, 1613.

The face is forceful and manly, and much more romantically handsome than the previous two, and the iconography is explicitly martial—he poses in armor, and in the right background are soldiers and tents, a military encampment. Figure 17 shows Prince Henry practicing at the lance, a popular engraving that appeared as the frontispiece to Michael Drayton's long poem about England's history and topography *Poly-Olbion*, published in 1613 and dedicated posthumously to the

Figure 18. Inigo Jones, *Prince Henry as Oberon* in Ben Jonson's masque *Oberon*, 1611. © Chatsworth Settlement Trustees

prince. This expresses more of the military idealization, and we note the imperial Roman profile again. And finally, Figure 18 is Inigo Jones's version of the prince in classical armor, in Ben Jonson's court masque *Oberon* on New Year's Day 1611, when he was not yet seventeen—this drawing was done less than a year after the investiture portrait of the slim youth in the fancy clothes. It hardly needs to be emphasized that the physical idealization here—the classic musculature, the commanding stance—is the work of the artist: this young man has not been pumping iron for the past six months.

The developing image is fully consistent with the role the prince imagined for himself. His plan had been to follow his sister Elizabeth to Bohemia after her marriage to the Elector Palatine, and to lead the Protestant armies against the forces of imperial Roman Catholicism. No doubt, had he lived, seven years later he would have wished to go to war in support of his brother-in-law's claim to the Bohemian throne, something that his pacifist father, dedicated to accommodations with the Roman Catholic powers on the continent, would certainly not have permitted the Prince of Wales to do.

Inigo Jones

Let us now consider Inigo Jones's own development. We have seen how Peacham considers Arundel's collection especially valuable for the way it functions as an education specifically for painters and architects, and for their potential patrons. But in a sense this gets things backwards, because Jones was as much the architect of all three of the collections we have considered as their beneficiary; he was the expert to whom first Prince Henry and Arundel and then Charles turned for the cultivation and legitimation of their taste. And this gives us our first inkling of how unexpected Peacham's use of aesthetic sophistication as the mark of a gentleman is: the arts were still very much crafts in Jacobean England. There is nothing comparable to the Italian notion that artistic ability rendered the artist godlike, producing "the divine Michelangelo." Nicholas Hilliard and Isaac Oliver are admired because they so completely fulfill the requirements of their employers; even in Charles I's time, the artists' union was still the Worshipful Company of Painter-Stainers, who had banded together in 1502, and were primarily active in attempting to prevent lucrative commissions from going to foreign workmen. In contrast, the Florentine artists by this time were calling themselves an academy, and insisting that painting was not a craft but one of the liberal arts, literally "arts worthy of a free citizen"—a gentleman. Inigo Jones was not a gentleman. He came into the artistic world precisely as a craftsman, the son of a London clothworker, trained as a joiner. He is first referred to not as an artist or even as a painter, but as a "picture maker," a producer of commodities. There is more than irony in the fact that his collaborator and adversary Ben Jonson's detractors were fond of reminding him that he had once been apprenticed to a bricklayer: the arts in England were still very much crafts. The changes in status came eventually, but only through the mediation of foreign artists: Rubens was Charles I's ambassador extraordinary, negotiating peace with Spain, not because he was a great painter, but because on the continent his artistic talent had given him an easy familiarity with the world of kings and courts; he was duly knighted, as, after him, was van Dyck. No English artist was treated in this way until Sir Peter Lely (and even he was originally Dutch).

So Jones really is a pivotal figure, not least in his deep and longstanding association with the aristocratic, snobbish Arundel, whose taste he was instrumental in forming; a crucial figure in the transformation of the artist, and the arts, and of artistic taste itself, in England. I turn now to what we may call Jones's own collection, the imagery that he appropriated and adapted to his own uses.

Figure 19 is the earliest of Jones's surviving stage designs, the House of Fame, for Ben Jonson's *Masque of Queenes,* performed at Whitehall Palace in 1609. This is, stylistically, a remarkably miscellaneous building to have come from the pen of the architect who was to introduce neoclassicism into England. A Roman arch below supports a Gothic trefoil above. Within the trefoil is a piece of stage machinery, a turning machine bearing the queen with eleven ladies on one side, and on the other the winged figure of Fame (she is visible in the minimalist sketch at the lower left). The façade is adorned with classical statues: on the lower tier are Homer, Virgil, and Lucan, on the upper Achilles, Aeneas, and Julius Caesar—these are not based on the Arundel marbles, which had not been acquired yet, but they spring from the same sensibility that found in classical sculpture the essential link between heroism and history on the one hand, history and taste on the other.

Figure 20 is the palace Jones designed for Prince Henry in *Oberon* two years later, in 1611. Again, the miscellaneous quality of the invention is striking: this is a veritable anthology of architectural styles. A rusticated basement seems to grow out of the rocks. The parterre has a Palladian balustrade. A splendid pedimented arch surmounted by a Michelangelesque figure fills the central façade, supported by grotesque Italian terms, and accented by Doric pilasters and Serlian windows (the Michelangelesque figure is not identified in Jonson's text—this is Jones's own evocation of his Italian avatar). The crenellated turrets of an English castle are topped with tiny baroque minarets; two pure

Figure 19. Inigo Jones, *The House of Fame*, from Ben Jonson's *Masque of Queenes*, 1609. © Chatsworth Settlement Trustees.

Elizabethan chimneys frame an elegant dome based on Bramante's *tempietto* in Rome. And here there seems to be a point, even a program, being enunciated; the inspiration is not merely eclectic. This design begins to make a claim about the national culture and the sources of its heroism: that England becomes great, a suitable context for the heroic young prince, through the imposition

Figure 20. Inigo Jones, *Oberon's Palace* in Ben Jonson's masque *Oberon*, 1611. © Chatsworth Settlement Trustees.

of classical order upon British nature; the rough native strength of the castle is remade according to the best models, civilized by the arts of design, by learning and taste. In the same way Prince Henry as Oberon emerges in classical armor from the woods, tames the rough satyrs who open the masque, and descends from the stage to salute his father, the real King James, at the center of the Palladian architecture of the Whitehall Banqueting House.

There are clear analogues to this in Jones's architectural thinking: for example, in the new façade he designed for old St. Paul's (Figure 21), combining ancient and modern Roman elements to refine and complete the venerable Gothic cathedral; or perhaps most strikingly, in his reconstruction of Stonehenge (see Figure 9), surely the most uncompromisingly British of ancient monuments, as a Roman temple in what he calls the Tuscan style. But the refining could also work in the other direction, with British strength restoring ancient virtue, and the essential material in this enterprise was classical allusion.

Figure 21. Inigo Jones, façade of old Saint Paul's Cathedral. From William Dugdale, *The History of St. Pauls Cathedral in London*, 1658.

In 1610 Jones staged a Barriers to celebrate the creation of Prince Henry as Prince of Wales. *Prince Henry's Barriers* opened in the ruins of the fallen House of Chivalry. Figure 22 is Jones's design for the setting. Amid this jumble are several identifiable ancient Roman structures—the pyramid of Caius Cestius, a bit of the Colosseum in the left foreground, Trajan's column on the right, the colonnade of the Temple of Saturn in the Roman forum, perhaps the arch of Titus in ruins at the back: all the allusions would have registered—they are quite standard, familiar from books of Roman antiquities, if not from visits to Rome. But note the surprisingly up-to-date little tomb in the lower left corner.

Figure 22. Inigo Jones, *The Fallen House of Chivalry*, for Ben Jonson's *Prince Henries Barriers*, 1610. © Chatsworth Settlement Trustees.

The architectural historian John Harris identified it as the base of a funeral monument Jones designed for a Lady Cotton in Shropshire around 1610 (Figure 23). So this setting as a whole says that chivalry is ancient and decayed, and that its history is specifically classical; it is the Roman ideal that has been allowed to die. But it also says, in the lower left-hand corner, that there is something that preserves that ideal in this world of ruins, and it is exemplified by Lady Cotton's authentically classical little monument—the classicism that lives on, or is restored to life, through Prince Henry's architect. This is an allusion that could have been recognized only by Inigo Jones himself, but it speaks volumes about his sense of himself.

Now comes the transformation scene, in Figure 24: Merlin appears as a star in the heavens, and summons the new prince to restore ancient chivalry

Figure 23. Inigo Jones, Detail from a design for a monument to Lady Cotton, St Chad's Church, Norton in Hales, Shropshire, ca. 1610. RIBA Collections, London.

Figure 24. Inigo Jones, Chivalry restored, for Ben Jonson's *Prince Henries Barriers*, 1610. © Chatsworth Settlement Trustees.

and make England its standard-bearer. Things now look a good deal better: there is still a fair amount of ancient rubble, but several of the monuments have been rebuilt—Trajan's column has a new capital, and a goddess atop it; the portico from the forum has been incorporated into a handsome renaissance façade; the ruined arch has been refurbished and moved, somewhat perilously, to the top of a cliff. At the center, leading to the restored House of Chivalry, is now St. George's Portico—not a restored building, but one newly minted: there appears to be no source for this elegant gazebo; it is one of Jones's few genuinely original stage buildings. And though it is arcaded, and has a dome, it is thoroughly gothicized, which is to say anglicized. It is basically a Gothic pavilion—Jonson's text describes it as an ancient monument "yet undemolished," but the ancient monument now is British, not Roman. The crenellated palace at the right and the little castle at the upper left repeat the theme—chivalry has moved to England.

But at the lower left, Lady Cotton's monument has become one of Michelangelo's Medici tombs (Figure 25). Thus Prince Henry, and his architect Inigo Jones, remake England according to the best models, classical, Italian, and English, and Jones is both the English Palladio and the English Michelangelo. As to the question of the audience for these allusions, if Jones is speaking to anyone at this point, it is surely basically to himself.

Chivalric architecture gets codified in Jones's setting for Jonson's *Oberon*, the Whitehall masque of the next year. The palace Jones designed for Henry as the Fairy Prince (in Figure 20) combines the elements of the Barriers setting into an elegant synthesis. Such settings stage the familiar through the imagination of otherness. But they also assert a control—or the illusion of one—over the phenomenal world that is denied to us in reality.

Sometimes, of course, the connoisseur's instinct leads not to synthesis but to direct appropriation. Figure 26 is the entry of Hercules's drunken cupbearer and two satyrs at the opening of Ben Jonson's masque *Pleasure Reconciled to Vertue*, performed at Whitehall in 1618. It derives, scarcely altered, from the Bacchic scene in Figure 27 engraved by Marcantonio Raimondi after a Roman sarcophagus. It is a little disappointing to find the splendid Whining Lover from *Loves Triumph Through Callipolis*, performed in 1631, deriving so literally from Callot

Figure 25. Michelangelo Buonarroti (1475–1564). Dawn: detail from the monument of Lorenzo de' Medici, Florence. Alinari/Art Resource, New York.

(Figures 28 and 29); or to find that the only thing original about the deliciously original Dwarf (or Dutch) Postman from Hell in *Chloridia* a month later is the chicken-footed horse (Figures 30 and 31).[18] In a sense all this is hardly worth remarking. All artists do this sort of thing; this is simply the nature of artistic invention—imitation is what art is all about. Especially in this era: as we have already observed, this is the age when Julius Caesar Scaliger told aspiring poets

Figure 26. Inigo Jones, Hercules's cupbearer and two satyrs in Ben Jonson's masque *Pleasure Reconciled to Vertue,*1618. (The two dancing figures on the right belong to the antimasque of the work's second performance, *For the Honour of Wales.*) © Chatsworth Settlement Trustees.

Figure 27. Marcantonio Raimondi after a Roman sarcophagus, Bacchic scene (detail). Engraving. Metropolitan Museum of Art, New York. Purchase, Joseph Pulitzer Bequest, 1917.

Figure 28. Inigo Jones, whining lover from Ben Jonson's *Loves Triumph Through Callipolis*, 1631. © Chatsworth Settlement Trustees.

Figure 29. Jacques Callot, Frontispiece, *Balli di Sfessania*, 1622. Metropolitan Museum of Art, New York. Bequest of Edwin De T. Bechtel, 1957.

Figure 30. Inigo Jones, dwarf postman from Ben Jonson's *Chloridia*, 1631—a note on the drawing refers to him as a Dutch postman. © Chatsworth Settlement Trustees.

Figure 31. Jacques Callot, Dwarf from *Varie Figure Gobbi*, 1616.

that although the function of art was to imitate nature, the best way to imitate nature was to imitate Virgil.[19] The only interesting point in Jones's copies, really, is what gets imitated; and that is what is new: English artists had never practiced this kind of imitation before—Jones's genius is all about deciding what the right models are. That is what he did for Prince Henry, Arundel, and King Charles too.

Here, finally, is a scene that we may read as Jones's tribute to his first and most faithful patron. Figure 32 is the Forum of Albipolis, for the 1632 masque *Albions Triumph*, in which the increasingly imperial King Charles presents himself, not for the first or last time, as a Roman emperor. The whole is thoroughly, splendidly classical. The architecture comes, however, not from Vitruvius or some other properly classical scholarly source, but from recent stage history: it is adapted from a Giulio Parigi design for an

Figure 32. Inigo Jones, the Forum of Albipolis, for Aurelian Townshend's masque *Albions Triumph*, 1632. © Chatsworth Settlement Trustees.

Figure 33. Remigio Cantagallina after Giulio Parigi, *The Temple of Peace*, one of seven interludes for the wedding celebration of Cosimo de' Medici in Florence, 1608. Etching. Metropolitan Museum of Art, New York.

interlude performed at a Medici wedding in Florence in 1608 and subsequently published (Figure 33). But the setting is also localized: David Howarth has recognized the first two statues at the head of the colonnades as two of the Arundel marbles, Caius Marius on the left, and on the right a draped Roman lady.[20] History was soon enough to reveal the imperial vision as hollow, something that could be maintained only in the world of court masques, but there is more than irony in the placing of Arundel's artistic vision at the forefront of an England idealized and restored. What politics could not effect, aesthetics did.

Let us consider, in conclusion, the astonishing remnant in Figure 34, the only surviving drawing of a Shakespeare play from Shakespeare's lifetime. It looks like a scene from *Titus Andronicus*, but in fact it combines a number of actions, and gives a conspectus or epitome of the play as a whole—it is accompanied by a text that combines material from acts 1 and 5.[21] This drawing is not an eye-witness sketch of Shakespeare on the stage; but it shows how

Figure 34. Henry Peacham (?), a scene based on *Titus Andronicus.* The caption reads, "Enter Tamora pleadinge for her sonnes going to execution." Reproduced by permission of the Marquess of Bath, Longleat.

a contemporary imagined Shakespeare in action, and is certainly informed by a theatergoer's experience. The costumes seem to us a hodgepodge, but they indicate the characters' roles, their relation to each other, and most important, their relation to us. A few elements are included to suggest the classical setting, but there is no attempt to mirror a world or recreate a historical moment. There are a Roman general, a medieval queen, two prisoners, and their guard in outfits that are a mixture of Roman and Jacobean; and the soldiers on the left, who are entirely modern.

The anachronistic details serve as our guides, accounting for the figures and locating them in relation to our world. We are always told that the Renaissance stage performed history as if it were contemporary, but an image such as this renders the claim untenable. On the contrary, the drawing provides a good index to the limitations on the imagination of otherness. Our sense of the other depends on our sense of its relation to ourselves; we understand it insofar as it differs from us, and conversely, we know ourselves through comparison and contrast, through a knowledge of what we are not—we construct the other as a way of affirming the self. The anachronisms here (and, indeed, throughout Shakespeare's drama), far from being incidental or inept, are essential; they are what locate us in history. The meaningful re-creation of the past requires the semiotics of the present. Anachronism is essential to the very notion of historical relevance itself, which assumes that the past speaks to, and is in some way a version of, the present. Sometimes it was a threatening version: hence Jonson's arrest over *Sejanus*, the suppression of the deposition scene in *Richard II*, the banning of John Hayward's *History of Henry the Fourth*. Nothing in the past is safely in the past, and the dark side of how productive classical models were was how dangerously pertinent—how alive—they could also be.

Chapter 5

From Black Letter to Roman

What Books Look Like

The look of the printed book changed significantly over the first century of its development. The pages designed by Gutenberg and Fust presented a dense black mass of type. For their early readers, these would not have been as forbidding as they appear to us, since printing did not represent the final form of the book. The page would have been completed in manuscript by the addition of capitals, generally in red and blue, and with running heads and sometimes marginal illustrations. Printing in such an enterprise was an intermediate stage in the preparation of the book, and early printed books required scribes and often illuminators, and on the part of the eventual owner a good deal of "perfecting" as well, both to make the book readable and to make it his or her own.

But printing soon began to incorporate what A. R. Braunmuller calls the transcription of space.[1] To begin with, legibility for all but the most expert readers requires spaces between words. The inclusion of these was a long time in coming—it was standard well before the invention of printing but came fairly late in the history of writing. More broadly, the transcription of space involves the development of a variety of aids to reading, the radical transformation of the page effected in printing by the addition of leading between lines and the division of the mass of type into paragraphs, verses, sections, or chapters. The changing look of the page reflected a significant change in the practice of reading—reading aloud, as it generally was until relatively recently. White spaces serve along with punctuation, which also developed only gradually, as guides, to indicate grammatical and rhetorical structure and pauses and emphases in speech: readers have increasingly required guides as literacy has required less and less expertise. Mark Bland describes the transformation as "the shift from the page as a solid block of text to a more open grouping of typographic elements: a series of changes that taken together might be described as 'the definitive triumph of white over black.'" This both produced and was a response to changes in the practice of reading.[2] The effect was continuous and incremental: we have only to compare the paragraphs of Sidney's *Arcadia*, which regularly extend to several pages, with those of Dickens, ten or fifteen lines long, and with those of any contemporary work of popular fiction, which sometimes barely exceed a single sentence. These changes also, of course, indicate the diminishing attention span of readers.

A book is not limited to, or defined by, its text. As we experience it, it has a binding, which may be very elaborate, flyleaves, half titles, sometimes frontispieces, title pages, tables of contents, and the whole range of material we call paratexts—preface, acknowledgments, notes, appendices, index: these make up a good deal of the book, but not of its narrative or argument. Without them, is the book complete or not? In fact, there is no agreement about what is and is not properly part of the book. Modern books have dust jackets, sometimes designed by famous artists. Publishers believe these attract purchasers, and therefore spend a good deal on their production; but they are ignored by bibliographers and routinely discarded by libraries. On the other hand, they are so highly prized by bibliophiles that a modern book without its dust jacket has lost a good deal of its value in the collectors' market. There is even a market for forged dust jackets, for titles like *The Great Gatsby* or *A Farewell to Arms*. Is the dust jacket part of the book or not? The answer will depend on whom you ask.

The title page, the introductory leaf whose sole function originally was to announce the subject of the book (though it now also identifies the author and publisher, and often but not invariably the date of publication, and on its verso information about copyright, editions, etc.), took several decades to develop.[3] The first title page that was not purely typographical but was also decorative, including an ornamental border, was designed for a 1476 Venetian

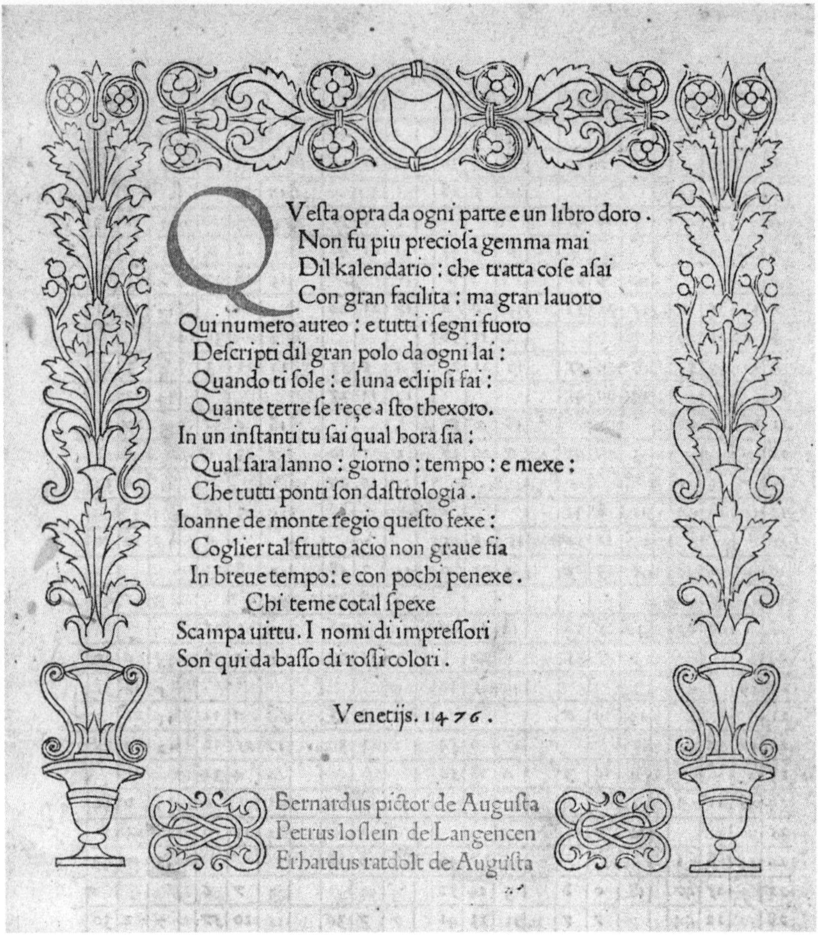
Veſta opra da ogni parte e un libro doro.
Non fu piu precioſa gemma mai
Dil kalendario : che tratta coſe aſai
Con gran facilita : ma gran lauoro
Qui numero aureo : e tutti i ſegni fuoro
Deſcripti dil gran polo da ogni lai :
Quando ti ſole : e luna eclipſi fai :
Quante terre ſe reçe a ſto thexoro.
In un inſtanti tu ſai qual hora ſia :
Qual ſara lanno : giorno : tempo : e mexe :
Che tutti ponti ſon daſtrologia.
Ioanne de monte regio queſto fexe :
Coglier tal frutto acio non graue ſia
In breue tempo : e con pochi penexe.
Chi teme cotal ſpexe
Scampa uirtu. I nomi di impreſſori
Son qui da baſſo di roſſi colori.

Venetijs. 1476.

Bernardus pictor de Auguſta
Petrus loſlein de Langencen
Erhardus ratdolt de Auguſta

Figure 35. Regiomontanus, *Calendarium*, Venice, 1476, title page.
Houghton Library, Harvard.

edition of Regiomontanus's *Calendarium,* an essential handbook providing calculations of the phases of the moon, eclipses, equinoxes, and most important, the date of Easter (Figure 35).

Before this, and afterward until the early sixteenth century, printers followed the standard form of the manuscript tradition for titles, a simple incipit. In manuscripts, this normally came at the top of the first page of text. Printed books, as they were produced in much larger numbers and underwent more handling, required more protection, hence the addition of an outer leaf. The incipit logically went there, producing a literal "title page." This was a practical matter, and decoration on the title page was not seen as an immediate improvement. Other information (the date, the name of the printer, a register of the gatherings for the binder, only very occasionally the name of the author) appeared at the end, in a colophon (literally "summit," hence, the end of the ascent through the book—the use of the term in this sense apparently dates from the eighteenth century). Of the 1476 *Calendarium* title, A. Hyatt Mayor writes, "This was a title page so modern that it listed author ['Ioanne de monte regio questo fexe'], title, place of publication, printer-publisher, and date in Arabic numerals."[4] The text, moreover, is in roman type, which had been introduced by the Venetian printer Nicholas Jenson in 1470, only six years earlier, for an edition of Eusebius. Mayor continues, "The surrounding frame is the first Venetian woodcut printed with metal type, and the earliest print of classical ornament."[5]

The look of this page thus may be thought of as strikingly modern but—or perhaps through—incorporating the ancient. It is to the point that the first ornament was classical and signaled a revisionist design: though all early printers were trained either in Germany or by printers trained there, book design in the southern countries soon abandoned the Gothic look for something that was recognized as more historically relevant, and therefore more elegant and authoritative. But it is also an indication of how relatively conservative book design was in the early years that the assertively beautiful title page took several decades to be adopted. From the beginning, and for several centuries thereafter, the external embellishment that declared the value and importance of the volume was not the title page, but the binding.

By the early sixteenth century Venetian presses were regularly using classical motifs on their titles; and in Basel, starting in the 1520s, Hans Holbein designed a variety of classicized title pages and borders for Swiss printers. Among the first were two versions of a very elaborate cartouche illustrating the Tablet of Cebes, a late classical ekphrastic work purporting to describe a painting depicting an allegory of human life—in other words, a world away from the simple decorative border of the Venetian *Calendarium*. These cartouches were used for a number of different books, first for a Greek Lexicon and a Tertullian, and thereafter for a New Testament, the works of Strabo, and a collection of Latin commentaries. As this indicates, the earliest decorative title pages, even when they involved pictorial narratives, had no necessary relation to the subject of the book. They were conceived as adornments, analogous to the elaborate tooled leather of modern fine bindings, which frequently encase books of no particular importance; or indeed, analogous to the splendidly carved and gilded frames for oil paintings, whose only relevance to the painting is an affirmation of its value.

English decorative title pages began later than those on the continent, and were on the whole, at least initially, less promiscuous. They also took longer to become stylistically classical. By the first decade of the sixteenth century, English publishers were regularly using title page illustrations that were directly related to the text; and in the next decade developed decorative borders for their titles—books printed on the continent for English clients (e.g., books of Hours for the use of Salisbury) were already using title page borders before the end of the fifteenth century. Wynkyn de Worde's titles often displayed, as the largest decorative item, not a scene from the narrative, but his own printer's device and his name. None of these employed specifically classical imagery; but Richard Pynson in 1523–1525, for various volumes of Robert Whittington's works on Latin grammar, used a border depicting a Roman triumph, including even a little elephant.[6] He also used it in 1523 for Thomas More's *Responsio ad Lutherum*, where it was more obviously celebratory.

The first Roman triumphal arch on an English title page was used, so far as I can tell, by William Rastell for a collection of judicial writs.[7] There is no obvious reason why this should have been classicized, though the arch may have implied to readers the dignity of the law; but Richard Grafton, issuing Chaucer's *Workes* in 1542, enclosed the title in a triumphal arch, and here the assertion of the classic for this ancient English poet was, if not intentional, at least logical and, in its historical context, significant: Chaucer was one of the few pre-Reformation English poets that Henry VIII's subjects were still allowed to read, despite his celebration of a pilgrimage to Canterbury and the erasure of Thomas Becket from the English martyrology. The arch, of course, may also be thought of as the frame of a funeral monument, and thus as much a memorial as a celebration.

For the 1561 Chaucer of John Wight, the poet was differently legitimized: there were alternative title pages, one with Chaucer's coat of arms (thus establishing his social status), the other displaying a frame surmounted by King Henry enthroned and surrounded by his councillors, with a pair of cherubs tending a grape vine and wine barrel below—the cartouche had first been used for the 1548 Halle Chronicle, to which it was certainly appropriate and for which it was probably designed, with the cherubs and wine implying both the fecundity of Henry's reign and the pleasures of reading about it. After that the cartouche adorned several issues of the statutes enacted in the first year of Edward VI, extending the authority of Henry to his son.[8] Its relevance to Chaucer may again lie in the fact that his works remained legitimate under the royal reforms. The second edition of Halle, in 1550, established Henry's dominion over reading matter even more forcefully: it surrounded its title with the Tudor genealogical tree. This cartouche was used again in Queen Mary's reign for a 1555 edition of Lydgate's Troy Book, another of the few pre-Reformation literary classics that had never been proscribed.[9]

Let us look ahead to a straightforwardly classical example, where the imagery is clearly part of the rhetoric of the book. Figure 36, the famous title page to Ben Jonson's *Workes*, 1616, constitutes a genuine collaboration between Jonson and the artist William Hole.[10] A triumphal arch frames the title, in Roman capitals, and the author's name, in a calligraphic italic, a stylized signature. On either side stand the figures of Tragedy and Comedy; above, the third of the classic genres, the satiric or pastoral is anatomized into the figures of satyr and shepherd. Between them is a Roman theater; above this stands Tragicomedy, flanked by the tiny figures of Bacchus and Apollo, patrons of ecstatic and rational theater respectively. On the base of the arch are two scenes illustrating the ancient sources of drama, the *plaustrum*, or cart of Thespis, with the sacrificial goat, the tragedian's prize, tethered to it, and an amphitheater with a choric dance in progress. The figures participating in both these originary scenes, however, in contrast to the classical figures above, are in modern dress—they are Jonson himself and his contemporaries.

This is a title page that is specifically designed for this book, a visual summary of Jonson's sense of his art, defining drama in relation to its history and

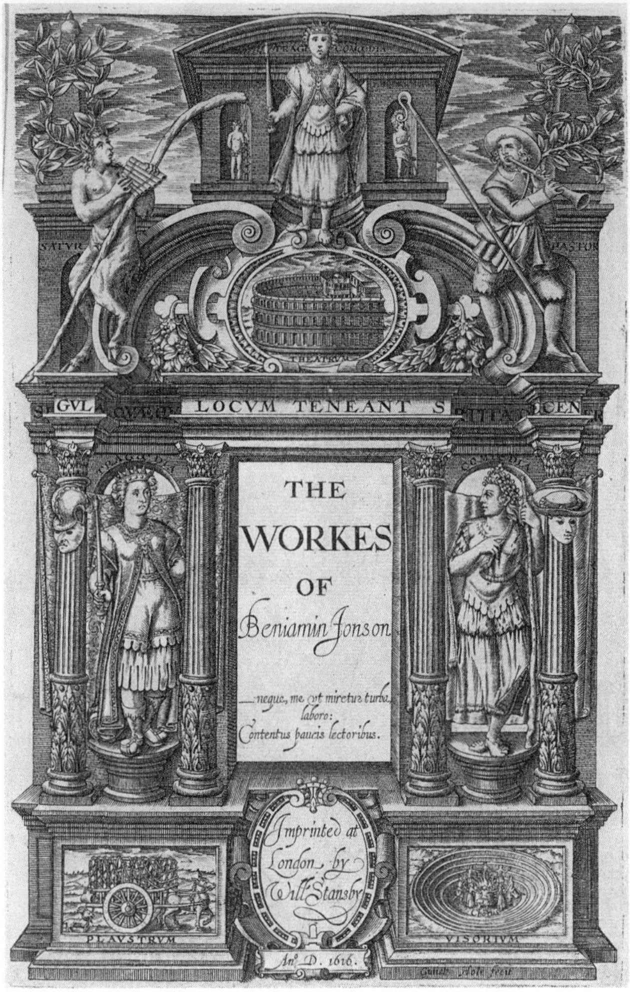

Figure 36. Ben Jonson, *Workes*, 1616, title page.
Folger Shakespeare Library.

its kinds, and postulating a set of generic possibilities. Visually, this is how Jonson presents himself, not with his own image—the book does not include a portrait.

Figure 37, Robert Vaughan's engraved portrait of Jonson, issued in 1626, was first included in the posthumous 1640 edition of *An Execration against Vulcan* and in the first volume of the 1640 collected Jonson; it was reengraved

Figure 37. Robert Vaughan, Ben Jonson, ca. 1626; used as the frontispiece to the 1640 folio *Workes.*

for the third folio of 1692. It was not until the eighteenth century that bibliophiles began adding it to the 1616 folio, usually as a way of completing an elaborate rebinding: these copies of the first folio are therefore essentially imitating the posthumous second and third folios, and also implying that something is missing. But nothing is missing—Jonson did not want his portrait in his book. In 1623, in the introductory poem to the Shakespeare folio facing its title page portrait, Jonson significantly urged the reader to "looke / Not on his picture, but his Booke."

The title page engraving for the Jonson folio would make no sense in any other book. It was not even used in the posthumous second volume, also published in 1640, where it would certainly still have been appropriate.

I turn now to an equally straightforward case in Figure 38, the title page of William Cuningham's *The Cosmographical Glasse*, 1559. This is a book about cosmography, cartography, and navigation, and the design both epitomizes and historicizes the work, again through a set of classical examples. At the top are three symbolic representations of time in relation to human life: Saturn, as Kronos/Chronos, personifies Time—the goat legs have never been explained, and are apparently unparalleled. I suggest that they constitute the same sort of etymological pun as Kronos/Chronos, fancifully etymologizing Saturn from *satyr*. Saturn leads the progression of mankind from childhood to maturity to old age. He is flanked on either side by sun and moon, day and night, including figures of youth and age, earth and sea. Below these are depicted famous ancient geographers and astronomers. At the bottom, around Mercury, patron of scholars, the quadrivium is anatomized in the figures of Geometry, Astronomy, Arithmetic, and Music.

This title page was designed for John Day, the publisher, possibly by the painter and engraver John Bettes (it is signed I. B.). It is comprehensive and specific, quite as specific to this book as William Hole's title page is to Jonson's, and equally difficult to imagine in any other context. And yet over the next sixty years it reappeared as the title page to an astonishing variety of other books. Day himself used it again only a year later, in 1560, for the *Works* of Thomas Becon, the Protestant divine. Thereafter he used it in 1564 for a commentary on the book of Judges, in 1570 for a Euclid, in 1572 for a volume on British ecclesiastical antiquities and in 1574 for the Acts of King Alfred. The woodcut then migrated to the printing house of Peter Short, who between 1597 and 1603 used it for books of ayres by Dowland and Rosseter, and for Morley's *Introduction to Practical Music*. It was then owned by Matthew Lownes, Short's son-in-law and heir, who used it in 1605 for the fourth edition of Sidney's *Arcadia* (Figure 39), and again in the same year for

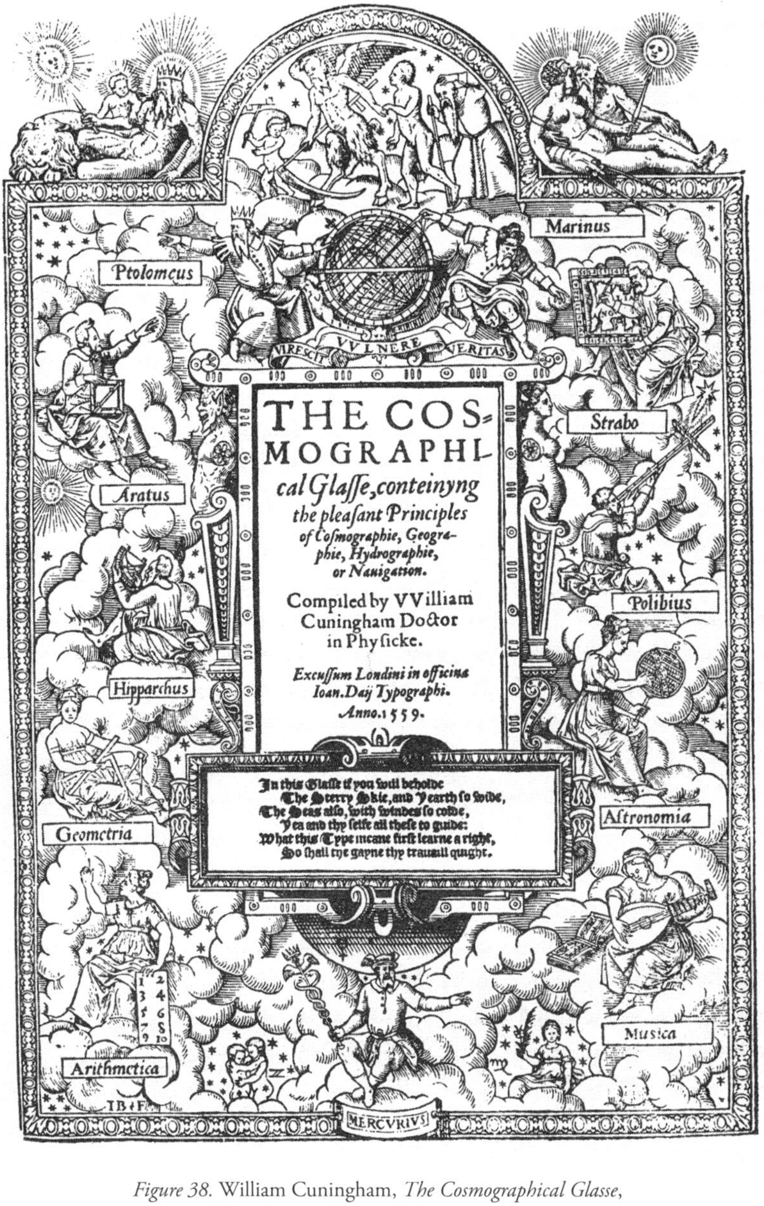

Figure 38. William Cuningham, *The Cosmographical Glasse*, 1559, title page. Folger Shakespeare Library.

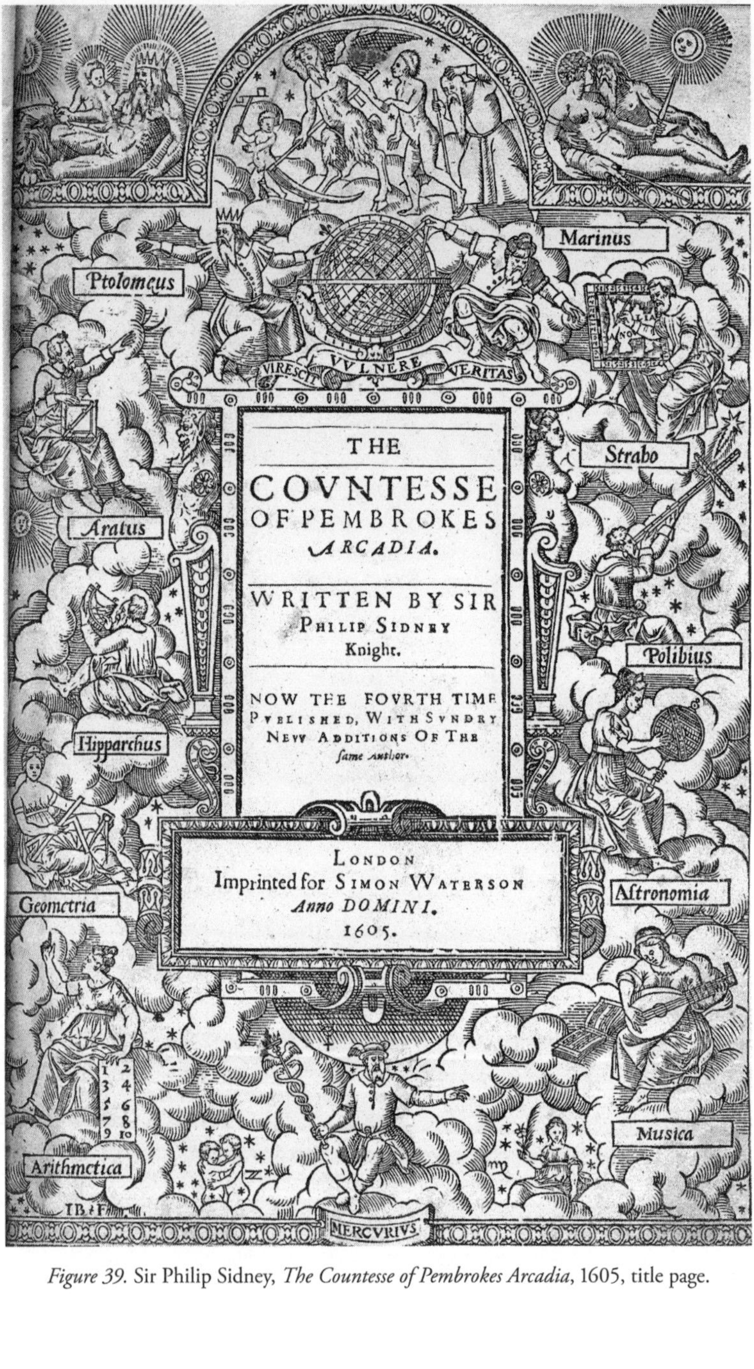

Figure 39. Sir Philip Sidney, *The Countesse of Pembrokes Arcadia*, 1605, title page.

Sternhold and Hopkins's *Psalms*. Between 1606 and 1613 Matthew's brother Humphrey Lownes used it three times for new editions of Dowland and Morley. In all, it was used as the title page for eighteen different works over more than half a century.

What does this mean—does it, indeed, mean anything? To begin with, the technology is a factor. As a woodcut, Day's cartouche is easily adaptable to the changing typography of new titles because woodcuts are printed on the press with the type. Engraved title pages like Jonson's must be printed separately, and changing their lettering involves reengraving the plate. But all this means is that reusing a woodcut title page is technically more feasible than reusing an engraved one: why did Day *want* to use this title for Becon, the commentary on Judges, and the Acts of King Alfred; why did the Lowneses want it for Dowland, Morley, the psalms and Sidney? The term for this use of illustration is "disjunctive"—that is, unrelated to the text—and it is generally taken to reflect the quality of the printing house. Since it is obviously a way of saving money, it is argued, bad printers will tend to do it and good printers will not. This explanation begs all sorts of questions (why are irrelevant illustrations a way of selling badly printed books?), but it really will not explain this case at all: Day, Short, and Humphrey Lownes were all perfectly respectable printers, and all their books are well produced (Matthew Lownes, a bookseller and publisher, not a printer, has been accused of shady dealings—e.g., literary piracy with regard to the 1597 *Astrophel and Stella*—but he was never sanctioned, and remained in business for three decades). The basic point in all these instances seems to be simply that large expensive books require elaborate title pages. The iconography is not critical, the elegance is. But then why commission symbolically specific title pages in the first place? Why not simply have a stock of decorative compartments, such as those designed by Holbein for his Swiss employers? And did a 1559 title page not look awkwardly old-fashioned in 1613?[11]

But on the other hand, is iconography really irrelevant? Here is another case, which appears to be a significant counterexample. Figure 40 is the title page for Sidney's *Arcadia*, 1593, the first folio edition. Its iconography relates it specifically both to the narrative and to Sidney. Classical figures of a shepherd

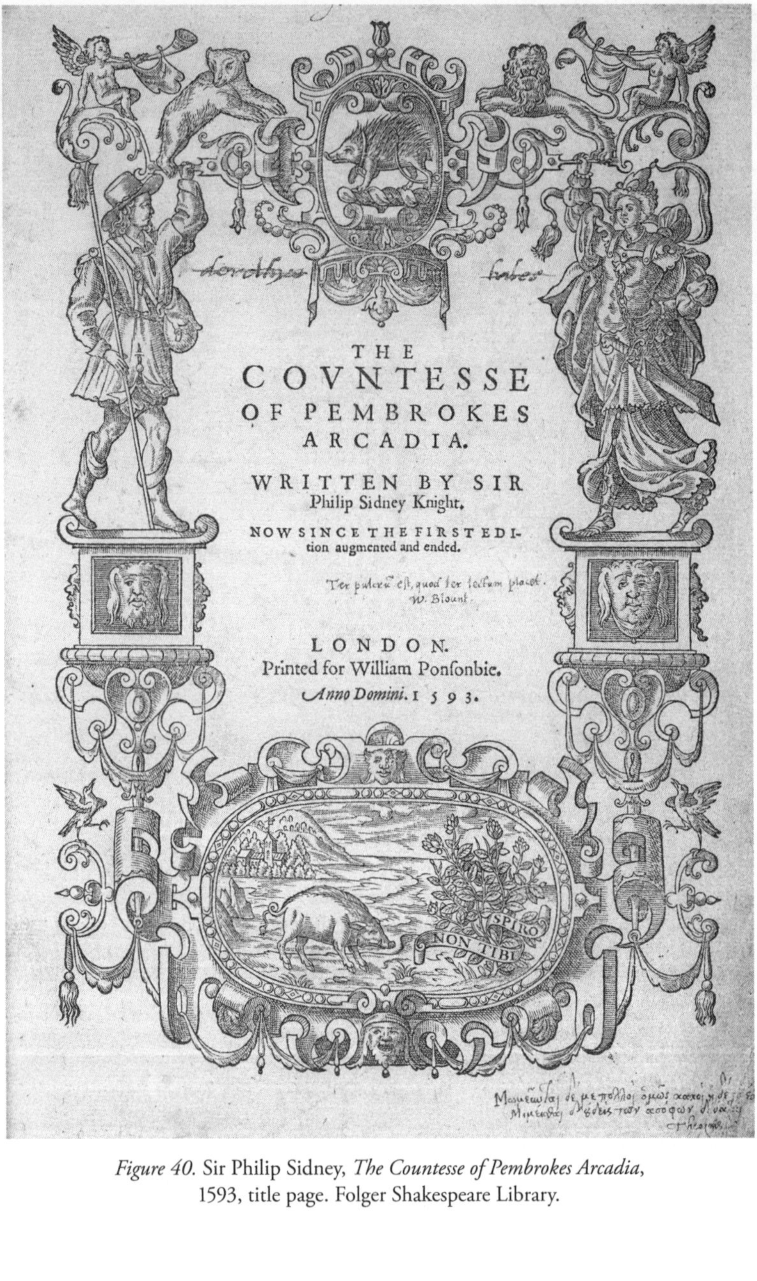

Figure 40. Sir Philip Sidney, *The Countesse of Pembrokes Arcadia*, 1593, title page. Folger Shakespeare Library.

and an Amazon flank the title: these are the heroes Mucidorus and Pyrocles in their romantic disguises as Dorus and Zelmane. Above them is a porcupine, the cautionary heraldic animal of Sidney's coat of arms. On either side are the lion and bear that, in an episode from book 2, threaten the heroines Pamela and Philoclea, and from which the disguised heroes rescue them. The emblem below, a marjoram bush announcing to an approaching pig *Non tibi spiro*, "my scent is not for you," gives the same warning Richard Tottel had given to prospective purchasers of *Songes and Sonnettes* in 1557, that the book is addressed only to readers of refinement.

Ponsonby used this title page again in 1598 for the third edition of *Arcadia*, and three decades later, long after Ponsonby's death in 1603, it resurfaced in the seventh and ninth editions of the book—in the fourth edition, 1605, we have seen that Matthew Lownes was using the *Cosmographical Glasse* title page for *Arcadia*.

In 1611 and 1617, however, Lownes used Ponsonby's title for the first folio editions of Spenser's works (Figure 41); and here the association of Spenser with Sidney certainly makes sense: *The Shepheardes Calender* had been dedicated to Sidney; *The Faerie Queene* is the poem that responds most clearly to Sidney's precepts in *The Defence of Poesie*, and if we think of Colin Clout and Britomart, shepherds and martial women are as relevant to Spenser's epic as to Sidney's romance. Sidney's coat of arms presides over Spenser's work as Sidney's writing informed the poet's endeavor.

But can we really conclude that the use of the title page here was deliberate? In 1595, between the second and third *Arcadia*s, Ponsonby himself used the title page for a translation of Machiavelli's *Florentine Historie*, and in 1625 Matthew Lownes was using it for the first comprehensive English version of Boccaccio's *Decameron*. Ten years later Humphrey Moseley attached it to a translation of Giovanni Francesco Biondi's romance *La Donzella Desterrada, or the Banished Virgin*. Is the woodcut's relevance to Spenser perhaps mere coincidence? And even if Lownes intended it to relate Spenser to Sidney, did any readers make the connection? In short, how did readers read title pages? Given the arbitrary nature of so many examples, did they ever regard them as anything other than decorative?

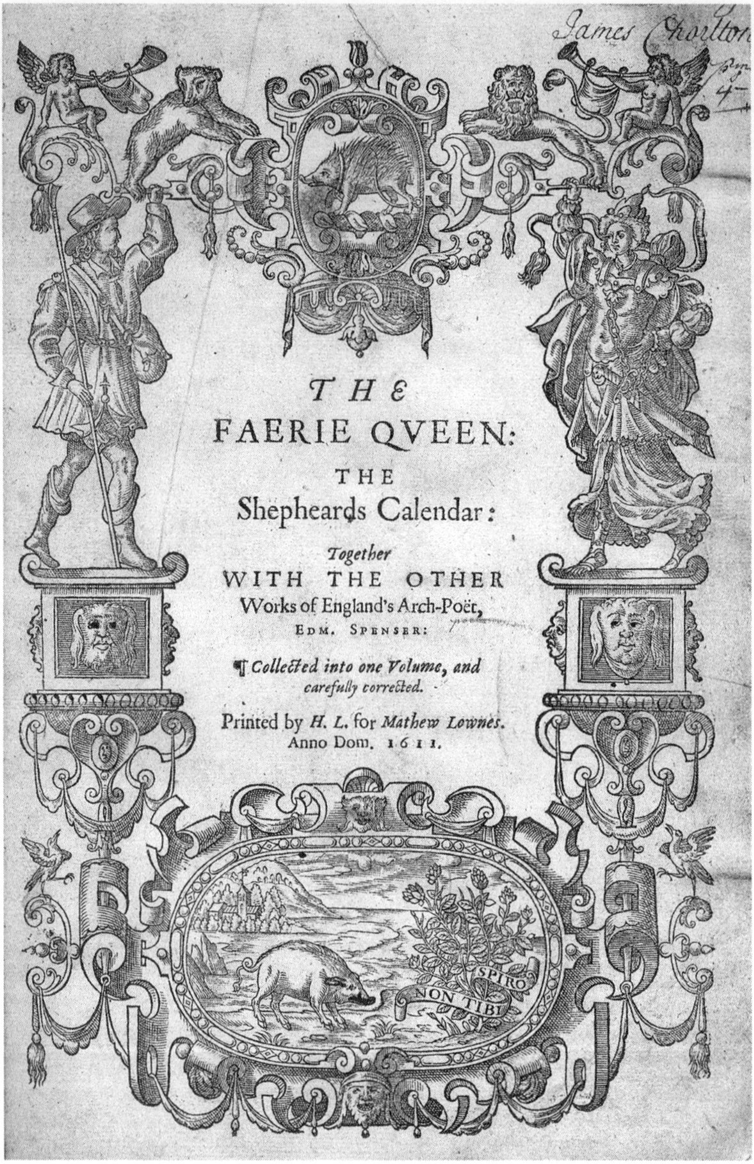
THE

FAERIE QVEEN:

THE

Shepheards Calendar:

Together

WITH THE OTHER

Works of England's Arch-Poët,

EDM. SPENSER:

¶ *Collected into one Volume, and carefully corrected.*

Printed by *H. L.* for *Mathew Lownes.*

Anno Dom. 1611.

Figure 41. Edmund Spenser, *Workes*, 1611, title page.

Typography

For the first four decades of printing in England, all books used the type Caxton introduced from Burgundy, a Norman-French version of what we now call black letter or textura, but which in the sixteenth century was called simply english. In 1509 Richard Pynson used roman type for the first time, for a heading in a Latin translation of a Savonarola sermon—the text of the sermon is in black letter—and in some sections of Alexander Barclay's *Shyp of Folys* (an English version of Sebastian Brant's *Narrenschiff* or *Stultifera Navis*), though the text of the work is also entirely in black letter. For the Latin *Oratio* of Petrus Gryphius in the same year, however, Pynson set the entire text in roman, and that shortly became standard for works in Latin. This is really very early, and was influenced primarily by the look of Italian printing: French printers were still using the gothic type that Caxton had imported into England, and did not switch to roman until the 1520s—*Champ Fleury*, Geoffroy Tory's splendid design for an elegant French roman type, was published in 1529. No classical text was printed in England in roman type until Pynson's edition of Cicero's *Philippicae* in 1521. The first work in English printed wholly in roman type was Leonard Digges's meteorological and astronomical treatise *A Prognostication of Right Good Effect* [. . .] *To Judge the Wether Forever*, 1555. The choice of typography for a text in English at this early date is striking: possibly it was designed to declare the credentials of the work—scientific and technical books were typically in Latin, and thus in roman type.

Consistency and systemization were a long time in coming. In 1514 Wynkyn de Worde published a Virgil *Bucolica* entirely in black letter. For the 1522 edition the text is in roman, with the commentary in black letter, even though the commentary is also in Latin. It is generally the case that from the 1530s to the 1590s, books in English printed in England have the body of the text in black letter, with roman or italic used for headings, notes, and the like. English printers use roman or italic for books in Latin, Italian, Spanish, or French, though there are interesting exceptions. John Stubbes's notorious *Discoverie of a gaping gulf whereinto England is like to be swallowed by another French mariage, if the Lord forbid not the banes, by letting her Majestie see the sin and punishment thereof*, published in 1579, is entirely in roman. This is an explosive tract, with no publisher or printer indicated. William Page was the publisher, Hugh Singleton the printer—Singleton otherwise invariably printed in black letter. Was the idea to pretend that it was a continental import, not the work of an English printer? If so, the ruse failed: author, publisher, and printer were immediately identified and punished. And George Puttenham's *Arte of English Poesie* published by Richard Field in 1589 uses no black letter at all. The text is in roman, quotations—in whatever language—in italic. Steven Galbraith observes that by the 1580s roman type was increasingly associated with the court, which may imply that the decision to use roman type for this compendious practical handbook to a courtly art was a way of soliciting an audience of aristocratic readers.[12] In the same year, Field printed Walter Bigges's *Summarie and true discourse of Sir Frances Drakes West Indian voyage* entirely in roman, but also printed *A true discourse of the discomfiture of the Duke of Aumalle* in black letter. Clearly the transition from old to new style was haphazard.

Nevertheless, some generalizations are possible. Italic was associated with speech, hence William Cuningham's *Cosmographical Glasse*, published in 1559, is mainly italic because it is a dialogue; and George Gascoigne's *Steele Glas* and *Complaint of Philomene* in 1576 are entirely italic and roman, with italic used for the voice of the poet in *The Steele Glas*, who also speaks in blank verse, and for that of Philomene, who speaks pentameter quatrains. But the fable of the rape and mutilation of Philomela and her transformation into a nightingale, which is in old-fashioned poulter's measure, are set in roman. Mark Bland observes that "the choice of italic marked the otherness of the text and the difference of voice; it linked the song of the nightingale with the eloquence of the poet, . . . witnesses to the survival of the past and the power of memory."[13]

Black letter continued to be used into the seventeenth century for literary texts associated with earlier eras: the works of Churchyard, Golding's Ovid, Phaer and Twine's *Aeneid*, Chaucer as late as the edition of 1687, are in black letter. Zachary Lesser points to an element of nostalgia in the occasional use of black letter in the seventeenth century.[14] Black letter was also felt to be more formal or official; thus bibles and edicts continued to be in black letter (as wedding invitations and funeral announcements frequently are today). The transition to roman type was not complete until the 1630s. Sabrina Baron writes,

"In the Elizabethan era, English printing, which had always lagged behind that on the Continent, continued to be for the most part in black letter, although roman was becoming more popular. Economics played a role here too; English printers used what type they had, and that was black letter. No type founders were working in England prior to the 1560s, necessitating expensive importation of type from the Continent. Subsequently, the shift to roman type in other areas of Europe made black letter cheaper and easier to acquire. So for reasons of economy and convenience, English printers held on to, and continued to use, their black letter as it was supplanted on the Continent. Black letter dominance in England was over, however, by the 1630s. Stanley Morison pointed out a gradual change over time as the result of a combination of factors, perhaps most importantly the growth of the reading public, in which more and better educated readers identified with roman type."[15]

As for the development of roman type, Baron goes on to claim that the Italian Renaissance and humanism "fostered a tendency to render the revived texts of antiquity in a script, and subsequently type, that closely resembled Roman carved inscriptions,"[16] but this cannot be correct. Roman carved inscriptions are all in capital letters; printed books include relatively few capitals, and the minuscules of roman type look nothing like Roman inscriptions, but derive from the uncials of the Carolingian monastic manuscript tradition—which may, of course, suggest a less pragmatic, more visceral reason for why Protestant England resisted roman type for so long. Even this, however, is not clear: the humanist developers of roman type based it on the handwriting of what they thought were classical manuscripts.[17] But also, Arthur Marotti observes, "One of the implications of the contrast between black-letter texts and roman texts is that the former was associated with the native literary tradition, whereas the latter was a classicizing mode: putting native vernacular verse in roman type, the form in which classical texts were printed, suggested that such texts were becoming canonized, monumentalized, set within a national literary tradition that was conceived as the continuation of a general literary tradition going back to such Latin poets as Ovid, Horace, and Virgil."[18] Moreover, printing Sidney and Spenser in roman in 1590 was bringing English literature definitively into the European Renaissance. Nevertheless, Chaucer—the unquestionable English classic—remained in black letter until the eighteenth century.

Illustration

The illustration of books was well under way before the invention of printing, and woodcut printing antedates the development of moveable type in Europe. Illustrated editions of Virgil and the Roman dramatists had appeared on the continent by the end of the fifteenth century, though no classical text printed in England was illustrated until the 1632 edition of George Sandys's translation of Ovid's *Metamorphoses*. In Europe, the illustration of such modern classics as the Nuremburg Chronicle, the Breydenbach *Peregrinatio in terram sanctam* and the *Hypnerotomachia Poliphili* are among the glories of early printing. Sometimes the illustrations, and more often initial capitals, were colored in by hand; in this respect printing was fully continuous with the manuscript tradition. Illustration is the most obvious index to how a work is imagined, though its usefulness as evidence is complicated by the fact that in many cases the same woodcuts were reused over many years, and new editions often copy illustrations from half a century or more earlier.

The later life of Caxton's illustrations to Chaucer are a case in point. I have discussed these in detail elsewhere; this is a brief summary.[19] When Caxton printed his second edition of *The Canterbury Tales* in 1483, he included twenty-two woodcuts illustrating the pilgrims described in the Prologue. These were reused or copied in subsequent editions issued by Pynson in 1492 and 1526, by William Thynne in 1532, and by John Wight in the Chaucer edited by John Stowe in 1561. The illustrations are as generic as pictures can be without being identical. From Caxton's versions on, many of the male figures, with the obvious exception of the knight, could be substituted for each other; and as for the women, though from Caxton through Thynne the Wife of Bath is definitively worldly, with a fashionable traveling hat and an inviting smile, in Wight's edition the Prioress and the Wife are the same woodcut, a demure religious figure, the feminine trumping the distinction between sacred and secular. By Thynne's edition of 1532, a single repeated woodcut was doing service for the Merchant, Summoner, Franklin, and Manciple.

But the Clerk of Oxenford is an interesting anomaly. In Chaucer his only passion is for his books, "Twenty bookes, clad in blak or reed / Of Aristotle and his philosophie." In Caxton's woodcut, however (Figure 42), he carries not

Figure 42. The Clerk of Oxenford from Caxton's Chaucer, 1483.
The Morgan Library and Museum, New York.

a book but a bow and quiver—he is clearly not an Oxford don. The figure is very similar to Caxton's Knight's Yeoman, for whom the bow and quiver are stipulated by Chaucer: "His arwes drouped nought with fetheres lowe / And in his hand he baar a mighty bowe" (107–8). Caxton, for whatever reason, had produced two versions of the Yeoman and used one for the Clerk. Pynson, in 1492, adapting Caxton's woodcuts, gave the Yeoman his bow and arrows, but also obviously saw the need to distinguish him from the similarly accoutred Clerk. The simplest way would have been to have the artist remove the Clerk's weapons and give him one of his beloved books; but that is not what Pynson did. Instead he commissioned the image in Figure 43, which retained the bow and quiver, but added a banner with the motto "The Scients"—the term means "The Liberal Arts." This is the only figure with a label, and it is supplied for him out of a felt need: because the image is both specific and wrong. But sincc the pictures are being recut anyway, why did Pynson not correct the image by simply replacing the weapons with a book? Why provide the label that contradicts the attributes? Because Pynson is following a double

Figure 43. The Clerk of Oxenford from Stowe's Chaucer, 1561.

and contradictory authority, Caxton and Chaucer. Nor does the progression end there: as late as 1561, John Stowe's edition reproduces versions of Pynson's woodcuts, with the Clerk carrying both his bow and quiver and his banner.

How then did readers read illustrations, if as realizations of the text they were inaccurate? It is clear in these examples that the important thing was the fact of illustration, not the accuracy of the depictions. Illustration served as an organizing and linking device, a kind of punctuation; as Martha Driver argues, print culture significantly expanded the functions images served in manuscripts.[20] Moreover, books have a history that is independent of their texts: John Wight's Stowe Chaucer looks back to Caxton, not to Chaucer; and by 1561 English artists were capable of far more sophisticated woodcuts than those that Wight reproduces, such as the *Cosmographical Glasse* frontispiece in Figure 38 above, or the complex and beautiful illustrations for John Heywood's *The Spider and the Flie* of 1556.

Caxton's woodcuts contribute a self-conscious archaism to the 1561 Chaucer. Similarly, the magnificent illustrations included in Sebastian Brant's edition of Virgil, published in Strasbourg in 1502, bring a sense of high chivalric style to the quintessential epic of love and war. These images were still being found appropriate by midcentury continental printers. This is always thought of as medievalizing Virgil, but perhaps it is more accurate to view it as preserving the conventions of a very famous book. In contrast, when Hugh Singleton needed suitably archaic illustrations for *The Shepheardes Calender* in 1579, he commissioned new ones that, for all their country simplicity, are devised in a style that accords with the book's elaborately modulated typography and testifies to the developing canons of Elizabethan taste—*The Shepheardes Calender*, after all, is the vanguard of a poetic revolution. But why is *The Shepheardes Calender* illustrated at all? Not because pastorals are illustrated—for the most part they are not—but because calendars are; and the very fact of illustration thus connects the book both with the newest continental poetry and with the most traditional of native forms, as does the book's mixture of black letter type with roman and italic.

Chaucer continued to be archaic not through illustration but through typography: Thomas Speght's two editions of 1598 and 1602 are printed in the now largely anachronistic black letter, which, as we have seen, was still being used for Chaucer as late as 1687. Speght's editions are bigger and better in that they offer additional poetry and a glossary of archaic words, but the real innovation is a sense of the author: they include a biography, a coat of arms, a family tree, and a portrait—in 1602, the portrait is engraved. The author portrait and the move to engraving are the real breaks with tradition here. Textually, however, the 1598 edition is so close a reprint of 1561 that it even repeats errors in folio numbering. As for the illustrations, Speght retained only Pynson's woodcut of the knight, a visible emblem of Elizabethan nostalgia for a chivalric past.

These editions indicate that claims for the revolutionary aspects of printing really do not take enough into account: books like Stowe's and Speght's Chaucer are profoundly conservative. So are the Spenser folios of 1611 and 1617, which carefully preserve the printing history of the 1590 and 1596 quartos, not only providing a new title page for *The Second Part of the Faerie Queene*, quite pointless for a one-volume edition of the whole work, but even retaining both sets of final dedicatory poems from the two quartos, thereby repeating three of them. Equally conservative, in their way, are the Shakespeare folios: the

1632 second folio is a page for page reprint of the 1623 first, even preserving the mistakes, such as the placement of the prologue to *Troilus and Cressida* before the title of the play—this despite the fact that there was also some very local editorial intervention: errors in Holofernes's Latin in *Love's Labour's Lost* are corrected. There are, no doubt, elements of both pedantry and ineptitude here;[21] but the point is the desire to replicate not simply the text but the physical book. Half a century later, in 1685, the fourth folio, with seven additional plays, still preserves the format of 1623.

Chapter 6

Staging the Classical

Beginnings

Around 1497 Henry Medwall, lawyer and ecclesiastic, a member of the retinue of the Archbishop of Canterbury, John Cardinal Morton, produced the play *Fulgens and Lucres* as an entertainment for the cardinal's court. This is the earliest surviving English secular play (that is, one not part of a religious cycle). It survives only because it was printed, sometime between 1511 and 1516, by John Rastell. It is set in ancient Rome, and concerns the choice of a husband by Lucres, daughter of the noble Fulgens, a Roman senator. Her two suitors are Publius Cornelius, a rich aristocrat, but also a wastrel playboy, and the virtuous, high-minded Gayus, a commoner of modest but adequate means. Initially Lucres asks her father to choose for her, but Fulgens leaves the decision to her, and it is to her that the contenders make their appeals. The play is based on a fifteenth-century Latin dialogue, *De vera nobilitate* ("On True Nobility") by the Florentine humanist and orator Buonaccorso da Montemagno (ca. 1428), which had been translated into English around 1460 by John Tiptoft, Earl of Worcester, and printed in 1481 by Caxton.[1] It is clear that the English translation was Medwall's source.

So English secular drama at the outset is classicized. Lucres's choice of the high-minded commoner over the sybaritic aristocrat is assumed to mirror the social world under Henry VII, in which the new aristocracy consisted of ennobled commoners who had succeeded by talent, energy, and loyalty to the regime. This is doubtless correct; but then what is the significance of the ancient Roman setting—why suddenly a classicized play? Greg Walker points out that "one significant factor was probably the popularity of the Latin drama published in both manuscript and printed form in the previous two decades. As humanist teaching methods found their way into the curricula of the English universities and schools, the plays of Plautus, Seneca, and particularly Terence began to find favour as set texts. Terence was taught at Cambridge from 1502, and at Oxford from some point after 1505. As early as 1483 Magdalen School, Oxford, had appointed a grammar master, John Anwykyll, who published a textbook which drew heavily upon Terence's comedies for its material for translation."[2]

And yet, so far as we can tell, *Fulgens and Lucres* is not part of a trend—the Latin drama of the universities and schools did not spawn a series of vernacular classics. The other English plays we know from the period are moralities, *Nature* (Medwall's one other play), *Hick Scorner*, *Everyman*, (probably) *Youth*. We need caution in generalizing, however: our only evidence is from the very small number of plays that were printed and of which copies have survived. The audience for *Fulgens and Lucres* in the form in which we have it would have consisted entirely of readers—and there is no reason to think that it was ever performed again. But in great houses throughout the realm, many plays would have been performed that no early publisher thought would find readers, and any number of these might have had classical settings. If, however, as Walker says, there was a sufficient market for Latin drama in print, why would there be no market for English drama in the classical style? There are possible answers to this question: perhaps the audience of Latinists was a different one, too small or too specialized, or exclusively interested in Latin—or at least, perhaps the printers working in England at the time believed this was the case. Or perhaps we should assume simply that there was no market *yet*—as with Surrey's blank verse, a general taste for classicized drama in English took some time to develop. Thus the first English drama on the Senecan model, *Gorboduc*, did not appear until 1560, about the same time that the first English Terentian and Plautine comedies *Ralph Roister Doister*, *Jack Juggler*, and *Gammer Gurton's Needle* appeared—these are works that are clearly indebted to the Latin plays students were reading in school.

Still, there is more to *Fulgens and Lucres* than *latinitas.* Much of the play does not take place in the classical world. There is a comic subplot of servants identified in the printed text simply as A and B, which opens in the present. These characters emerge from the audience—they are attendants at the banquet at which the play is to be performed—and summarize the plot. Then, as the drama of Lucres's choice of a husband begins, A and B enter the play's action, becoming the servants of the two suitors; and B undertakes, crudely (and unsuccessfully), to woo Lucres's maid. It is thus the modern English comic characters who are indebted to Plautus and Terence, not the serious ancient Roman ones. The servants parody the action, but also precede it—indeed, at one point in the plot summary when A protests that B will spoil the play, B replies sharply that the play has not started yet. This is a far more complex metatheatrical structure than would be found in English drama for another century (in, e.g., the frame stories of *The Taming of the Shrew* and Peele's *The Old Wives' Tale*).

A and B are not, of course, the two servants' names: their names are never mentioned in the dialogue. The speech headings merely distinguish them; they are a function of publication—for the purposes of performance, these characters do not require names. But there is a different sort of vagueness about the third servant, the maid: she is called Jone three times in the dialogue, and all modern commentators refer to her as "Joan"; but in the speech headings her name is An. For the purposes of the drama, identity is fixed only in the classical world—only the past is history. The play in fact has some fun with the names, or the lack of them: when Lucres asks B what his name is and whom he works for, he has forgotten both.

Moreover, the account they give of the play to be performed gets the action wrong. B tells A that the decision about which of the two suitors is the worthier will be referred to the senate, which will choose Gayus—in Montemagno's dialogue, the two suitors do make their arguments before the senate, but the text then says that the final judgment is not recorded (it is clear, however, that the virtuous commoner is set up to win). In the play, the suitors plead their cases directly to Lucres, who initially does not declare her choice; she says she will ask for advice, and then write her decision to the two men. Subsequently, however, she tells A and B that she has chosen Gayus. The play, that is, does not follow the announced plot. In performance this might not have been noticeable: the play is long, and was performed in two parts with a dinner in between. The final judgment would have come several hours after B's plot summary; moreover, the outcome is never in doubt. But is Medwall perhaps making the play independent of its plot, implying once again that the action is "really" taking place?[3]

Daniel Wakelin observes that in the world of Henry VII, the terms of the debate between old aristocracy and new merit were entirely familiar. The debate is really not a debate: it is designed to flatter the listeners, who are asked to give a judgment that is essentially a judgment about their own excellence.[4] In this reading, there were no surprises in the arguments; all the surprises were dramatic. Nevertheless, Medwall is extremely cautious, insisting several times that he is not enunciating general principles; that Lucres's decision refers only to the specific cases at hand, and should not be taken to reflect on anyone else present—anyone in the audience. Clare Wright therefore takes the opposite line from Wakelin: "Medwall, then, presented a highly controversial subject to his audience, many of whom were likely to be members of the aristocracy, and perhaps this accounts for the tentative nature of the play, its many disclosures, apologies, and diversions designed to mollify potential objections to its outcome."[5]

Both these views seem to me partly correct. Whether the outcome would have been found offensive or not would depend on who was in the audience: were Cardinal Morton's guests all new men like him (Morton came from a family of middling gentry)? Were some of them old aristocrats? If so, the striking thing would be both how obviously loaded the case is—something the hereditary nobility would surely resent—and the fact that Lucres does finally announce her decision: the decision in Medwall's source, the Montemagno dialogue, is implied but never stated. For Medwall, in any case, there would have been ways of leveling the playing field if that is what he had wished to do, presenting Lucres, and the audience, with a real choice. The aristocratic suitor need not have been a wastrel playboy. He might instead have been a person of high rank who uses his wealth and position for good ends. Alternatively, in the world Medwall inhabits, however unsavory Publius Cornelius's character might be, Lucres's father might well prefer an alliance with an old aristocratic family to one that merely provides his daughter with a high-minded husband—another reason for Medwall's caution against generalizing Lucres's choice. Daughters are marketable properties; thus Lucres (that is, Medwall) initially leaves the choice of the husband up to her father: the decision does not affect Lucres alone, but has implications for the position of the family as a whole. That such an argument is not admitted into the debate makes it clear which side Medwall expects his audience, and his patron Cardinal Morton, to be on; but he is also taking few chances, playing it very safe. This is modeling ancient Rome on Henrician England, not the other way round. Or more precisely, the model that is being revised and interpreted is that of ducal Italy in the fifteenth century. Rome is there to provide a superficial validation, but Medwall urges us not to extract doctrine from the dramatic fiction.

In fact, the play is only superficially and intermittently Roman. Montemagno's dialogue is set in Rome, but as we have seen, half the play's characters do not derive from the dialogue; they are English, and two of them are anonymous. A and B begin outside the fiction and then enter the world of the play; Lucres's maid Jone/An moves as well in both worlds. The Rome of the main plot is presumably Republican (there is a senate but no emperor), and Lucres is a classic model of virtue, recalling the Lucrece in the story of Tarquin and Lucrece; but why is the play titled *Fulgens and Lucres*? Fulgens is Lucres's father, and he has nothing to do with the drama beyond saying he will let his daughter choose for herself—calling the play *Fulgens and Lucres* is rather like calling *Romeo and Juliet* "Capulet and Juliet." Surely this is Medwall again playing it safe: whatever the outcome of this dramatic debate, daughters belong to their fathers, and the position of the father determines the desirability of the daughter. This Rome is very modern.

Classical Models

As I have indicated, the striking thing about *Fulgens and Lucres* is less its priority as a neoclassic drama than its uniqueness. The next plays in English on the classical model do not appear until half a century later—or at least, it is not until then that publishers decide that such plays are worth printing. Even then, there is considerable uncertainty about how to market plays: are the purchasers presumed to be performers who need scripts; people who have seen the play and want a record of it; people who were unable to see the play (e.g., in a performance at a court such as that of the archbishop of Canterbury) and want to know what they missed; people who like plays and want to imagine a performance; or simply people for whom drama is literature, and will read the play as they read anything else, for information, wisdom, entertainment?

By the time publishers were regularly issuing plays, the assumption was for the most part that there was nothing to do with modern drama but perform it, as *Jack Juggler*, printed in 1562, is declared on its title page to be "A newe Enterlude for Chyldren to playe."[6] For three decades in the mid-sixteenth century, published plays characteristically solicited performance by announcing, either on the title page or in the cast list, how many actors were required and how the parts were to be divided. "Foure may playe it easely," says the printed text of William Wager's interlude *The Longer Thou Livest the More Foole Thou Art*, published around 1568, and even supplies a chart distributing the fifteen roles among four exceptionally adaptable players. However, a thoughtful audience of readers is also solicited by the title page, which characterizes the play as "a myrrour very necessarie for youth, and specially, for such as are likely to come to dignitie and promotion." Academic plays like *Gammer Gurton's Needle* and *Ralph Roister Doister* are overtly literary, domesticating the Roman comedy taught in schools. As we have seen, Nicholas Udall, the playwright of *Ralph Roister Doister*, had even published an en face translation of selections from three Terence plays as a Latin conversation book, *Floures for Latine spekynge selected and gathered oute of Terence*; so for this playwright the boundary between reading and performance was essentially nonexistent.

Until the middle of the century, with the partial exception of *Fulgens and Lucres*, the classical models seem to have been exclusively comic. English tragedy on the Senecan or Euripidean model begins to appear only in the 1560s, and even these were not controlled by their exemplars. Sidney considered this a defect (*Gorboduc*, he says, is "defectious in the circumstances"), but what critics and theorists primarily wanted from the ancients was a set of rules, not a canon of vernacular classics. That playwrights for the popular theater had other interests goes without saying, but even self-proclaimed classicists such as Marlowe and Jonson ignored the rules—in the preface to *Sejanus*, Jonson apologizes for his defections, though largely as a way of advertising his awareness of them. Plays written for performance by schoolboys, such as Lyly's, often took as their subject matter stories from the classics, but rarely observed the rules derived either from Horace or from the drama the boys were studying. Latin academic drama, of course, was another matter, but even here the most prolific university playwright, William Gager, writes in the preface to his Oxford tragicomedy *Ulysses Redux* (1592): "I have produced this tragedy, or play, or historical narrative, or whatever it is right and proper to call it, not according to the exacting standards of the *Art of Poetry* employed as some sort of goldsmith's balance, but rather measured according to the exacting standards of popular taste."[7] The concessions to popular taste included a Latin that was more colloquial than formal, violent action presented on stage rather than reported (such as Ulysses's slaughter of Penelope's suitors: the slaughter takes place behind closed doors, but a stage direction calls for the sound of "terrific commotion" and drum beats "in order to preserve decorum," after which the doors are opened revealing the carnage), and a disregard of the unity of time. The play has more in common with *The Jew of Malta*, *Richard III*, and *Titus Andronicus* than with Seneca. It also includes a good deal of music. Gager's proper tragedies observe the rules, though Francis Meres cites him as among the best of the modern poets for comedy—his one known comedy, *Rivales*, has not survived.

In fact, whatever the theorists argued, the genres were never really separate. Socrates at the end of the *Symposium* tells Agathon and Aristophanes, tragic and comic dramatists, that their crafts are essentially the same. Heavy weather has been made of this, but there are many cases where it is almost self-evident—for Jonson in *Sejanus*, for example, the scheming and trickery at the heart of comedy is also the essence of tragedy;[8] and it has often been observed that plays like *Othello* and *Richard III* (and in ancient drama Euripides's *Bacchae* and Seneca's *Thyestes*) include much that is essentially comic.

English classical drama flourished at the schools and universities; but as Gager observes, even academic drama was responsive to the "standards of popular taste"—in this case, the populace consisted of the scholarly, largely upper-class performers and spectators, but their taste was still a problem for the classical norms. Of academic plays, the most famous is *Gorboduc*, which earns its place in the literary histories as the first English tragedy on the Senecan model. *Gorboduc* was written for performance at the Inns of Court and before the queen, and in that respect, it is not Senecan. The consensus of modern scholars is that Seneca's plays were not written to be staged, but to be read or recited. The evidence for this is both negative and positive: there are no ancient references to the plays being performed, no Roman actors celebrated for their interpretations of Senecan roles; and the heavily rhetorical nature of the plays themselves seems to preclude performance. The former evidence is more persuasive than the latter, which only reflects changes in taste. James I's favorite play, George Ruggle's *Ignoramus*, presented before him twice at Clare College, Cambridge, has very long speeches in Latin and took six hours to perform. Walter Montagu's *The Shepherd's Paradise*, written for performance by Queen Henrietta Maria and her ladies, had even longer speeches in English. There were complaints about the length from the aristocratic performers, but only the queen's opinion mattered, and the project went ahead. It was eventually performed in a somewhat cut version, but still lasted "seven or eight hours," according to a member of the audience writing after midnight on the night of the event.[9] In both these cases, taste is an issue, but popular taste is not—and if Nero had wanted to see Seneca's plays performed, they would have been performed.

Gorboduc is certainly Senecan in its long, sententious speeches; and when we characterize the play, those are what we focus on. But a contemporary account of the first performance gives a quite different sense of the work:

> Ther was a Tragedie played in the Inner Temple of the two brethren Porrex and Ferrex K[ings] of Brytayne betwene whome the father had devyded the Realme, the one slewe the other and the mother slewe the manquil[e]r [i.e. the manqueller or man-killer]. It was thus used. Firste wilde men cam[e] in and woulde have broken a whole fagott, but could not, the stickes they brake being severed [i.e. the first dumb show]. Then cam[e] in a king to whome was geven a clere glasse, and a golden cupp of golde covered, full of poyson, the glasse he caste

> under his fote and brake hyt, the poyson he drank of [the second dumb show], after cam[e] in mom[m]ers [the fourth dumb show]. The shadowes were declared by the Chor[us] first to signyfie unytie, the 2 [i.e. second] howe that men refused the certen and toocke the uncerten, wherby was ment that yt was better for the Quene to marye L[ord] R[obert] knowen then with the K[ing] of Sweden. The thryde to declare that cyvill discention bredeth mo[u]rning. Many thinges were handled of mariage, and that the matter was to be debated in p[ar]liament, because yt was much banding [very contentious] but th[at] hit ought to be determined by the councell. Ther was also declared howe a straunge duke seying the realme at dyvysion, would have taken upon him the crowne, but the people would none of hytt. And many thinges were saied for the succession to put thinges in certenty.[10]

The focus of this spectator was on the dumb shows—indeed, this account describes the three pantomimes as preceding the drama as a whole, rather than as preludes to the individual acts. This may, of course, reflect only the reporter's method of summarizing, but it is to the point that for this spectator, the meaning of the work was conveyed through the dumb shows and the chorus, not through dialogue and action. *Gorboduc* in this report sounds more like a traditional mumming than like Senecan rhetoric.

Moreover, the account of the dumb shows does not accord with the dumb shows described in the published text—these are two different plays. As we read *Gorboduc*, the play's meaning is quite general, having to do with keeping the commonwealth intact through securing the succession should the monarch die without issue. But for this spectator at the original performance, its meaning was quite specific. The queen was being counseled to marry her domestic suitor Robert Dudley, not the foreign suitor, the king of Sweden. The interpretation of the second dumb show in particular differs significantly from that given in the printed text. When our spectator saw the play, the chorus explained the contrast of a harmless clear glass and a golden cup containing poison as being about marriage with the known versus the unknown (the unknown, the king of Sweden, was poison); whereas in the surviving text, the chorus says it is about good counsel versus flattery. Marriage is not an issue anywhere in the play as it was published; but at the original performance, "many thinges were handled of mariage." The book we have was not the play the first audience saw.

By 1565, when *Gorboduc* was first printed by William Griffith, the Swedish king was no longer a suitor, and public discussion of the queen's marriage was increasingly discouraged. In order to be licensed, the play would have had to be revised for publication, and the marriage material would obviously have had to go. But it is likely that it was revised even for its second performance, the one before the queen, since the manuscript that was Griffith's copy apparently did not come from the authors, but was in circulation, and would have been a text originating in the script. There is nothing anomalous about this: plays are by their nature unstable, subject to constant revision according to the changing audience and the conditions of performance or publication.

In a culture of routine and pervasive censorship, nothing printed can be assumed to have been unaffected by anticipation of the censors and untouched by the licensing authorities. The second edition of the play, issued by John Day in 1570 under the title *The Tragidie of Ferrex and Porrex*, claims not only to have corrected numerous errors in the earlier text, which is said to be corrupt, but also to be "set forth without addition or alteration but altogether as the same was shewed on stage before the Queenes Majestie." Both these claims are demonstrably false: there is nothing corrupt about Griffith's 1565 text, which includes few evident errors; moreover, the textual differences between the two editions are infrequent and insignificant. Day's only major revision was to delete a politically charged eight-line passage from V.i. That is, Day's edition is *less* complete and accurate than Griffith's, and it certainly is not the play as it was performed before the queen. (The deleted lines declare that there are no grounds for rebellion against a legitimate monarch, even a tyrannical or criminal one—the position is perfectly orthodox, but it may have been felt to raise an issue that in itself was dangerous.) Day's version of the play was, moreover, clearly set up not from a new manuscript, but from a copy of the 1565 volume, lightly marked up—the basis for Day's text was the allegedly incorrect one.[11]

In short, *Gorboduc* looked Senecan only to readers. It is indicative that Sidney in the *Apologie for Poetrie* complained that the choruses were insufficiently classical, but took no notice of the dumb shows, which of course were not classical at all. In the literary histories, *Gorboduc* and Gascoigne and Kinwelmersh's *Jocasta* are the only English tragedies considered properly classical before Marlowe's *Dido Queen of Carthage*, which is generally treated as seriously flawed. But there were many classical tragedies in the period; they are largely ignored because most were in Latin. It is difficult for us now to recognize the real vitality of neo-Latin drama in Renaissance Britain. Its audience—an audience first of performers and spectators, then of readers—was relatively small, but it was elite and powerful; and plays like George Buchanan's *Jepthes* and *Baptistes*, Thomas Watson's *Antigone*, William Alabaster's *Roxana* had a real place in the political and ethical debates of the age. These dramas were certainly intended as literature, but they were performed and, although many remained in manuscript, a number were also printed.

As to those plays that have been called "closet drama"—generally explained as drama not intended for performance, but more properly in this period, drama in private settings—an audience of readers or an amateur performance was all very well for aristocratic authors like the Countess of Pembroke and Elizabeth Cary, Lady Falkland, but for writers without independent means or a generous patron, the acting companies paid much better than publishers of plays; and of course circulation in manuscript (the usual mode of publication for plays) did not pay at all. Hence Samuel Daniel's *Cleopatra* was initially written for the household of his patron the Countess of Pembroke, and was clearly intended as a companion piece to her *Antonie*, a translation of Robert Garnier's *Marc-Antoine*.[12] But a decade later Daniel reworked the play for the public stage. The standard modern critical assumption that only plays for the popular theater are worth attending to leaves one quite unprepared for how impressive Daniel's original *Cleopatra*, Pembroke's *Antonie*, Cary's *Mariam*, Fulke Greville's tragedies (to say nothing of *Samson Agonistes*) are to read. Moreover, we should bear in mind that though these plays were not destined for the playhouse, they were designed, if not for private performance, to be recited or read aloud, which was by far the commonest mode of presentation of all literature (not just drama) before the present. Recitations and readings are performances.

We would do well to reconsider our categories. The whole idea of closet drama as a separate genre in the early modern period appears increasingly questionable, and the popular and the elite have more in common than we have allowed. The two poles are represented by *Gorboduc*, formal and serious, and *Cambises*, declared on its title page to be "a lamentable tragedie, mixed full of plesant mirth," published 1569, and very obviously catering to the popular taste for variety. But *Cambises* was written by Thomas Preston, scholar and fellow of King's College, Cambridge, later Master of Trinity Hall, and vice-chancellor of the university. E. K. Chambers considered the play thoroughly disreputable, and declared its prosody doggerel—what Marlowe, inventing a new language for popular theater, was to call "jigging veins of rhyming mother-wits." Chambers even proposed that *Cambises* had been written not by the Cambridge scholar but by a hack of the same name. It was *Cambises*, and the myriad dramas in the same style, that Marlowe and shortly, Shakespeare, Jonson, Dekker, Fletcher, Middleton, Massinger, and all the other playwrights who make up what for us is the canon of English Renaissance drama—superseded, and effectively banished from the literary histories.

To Elizabethans, however, *Cambises* and *Gorboduc* had much in common; and both were performed at court in the season of 1561–1562 before the queen and an elite, well-educated audience.[13] The prosody of *Cambises*, which for Chambers was doggerel, was the classic fourteener couplets of Phaer, Golding, and Chapman's *Iliad*. It was also the prosody of all but one of the plays collected by Thomas Newton and published in 1581 as *Seneca his tenne tragedies, translated into Englysh*—seven of the translations had appeared individually in the 1550s and 1560s.[14] English Seneca, that is, sounded more like *Cambises* than like *Gorboduc*; and though no one would call Preston's prosody nuanced, the fourteeners sound more respectable if they are read aloud. Here are a couple of samples, in modernized spelling:

(A wicked judge)

Even now the king hath me extolled and set me up aloft;
Now may I wear the bordered gown and lie in down bed soft.
Now may I purchase house and land, and have all at my will,
Now may I build a princely place my mind for to fulfill.
Now may I abrogate the law as I shall think it good.
If anyone me now offend, I may demand his blood.

(A son whose father has been unjustly condemned to death addresses Fortune—the alliteration, which sounds comic to us, is characteristic of midcentury English prosody.)

> O false and fickle frowning dame that turneth as the wind,
> Is this the joy in father's age thou me assign'st to find?
> O doleful day, unhappy hour, that loving child should see
> His father dear before his fact thus put to death should be.
> Yet father, give me blessing thine, and let me once embrace
> Thy comely corpse in folded arms, and kiss thy ancient face.

As Sackville and Norton used the dumb shows of popular entertainment to underline their play's political message, Preston used the comic Vice Ambidexter and the burlesque trio Huf, Ruf, and Snuf to leaven his play's ethical and moral exempla. If we focus exclusively on the low comedy elements of the play and dismiss its fourteener couplets as doggerel, we ignore its humanist erudition and ethics—Ivan Lupić gives a shrewd and revealing reading of the two plays in tandem.[15]

Thomas Kyd is remembered today as the author of the popular blockbuster *The Spanish Tragedy*, but the only play published under his name in his lifetime was *Cornelia*, a translation of Robert Garnier's very formal Senecan drama *Cornélie.* It appeared four years after Mary Sidney's translation of Garnier's *Marc-Antoine*, and both plays were reissued in new editions in 1595. Clearly there was no great gap between the intellectual worlds of the popular dramatist and the elite countess. Moreover, in many cases, what looked classical to the Elizabethans is not what looks classical to us: though *Titus Andronicus* is in Marlovian blank verse (the new "classical"), it appears to modern eyes a fantasia of untamed rhetoric, with nothing classical about it except the setting, and even that has no identifiable source. But in fact, it is imbued with the classics, not only Ovid's *Metamorphoses*, which figures so significantly in the plot, but also the *Thyestes* and *Medea* of Seneca. To the Dutch traveler Johannes de Witt in 1596, English theater itself looked classical: he went to a performance at the Swan in London, and wrote home that Roman theater had survived in the English playhouse.[16]

Small Latin and Less Greek

The classical Shakespeare is, of course, heavily mediated; his mythology owes as much to Renaissance mythography as to Ovid, and his Plutarch could not have been consulted in Greek. But in *Julius Caesar*, Brutus's and Antony's funeral orations show a keen sense of classical styles, the coldly formal prose periods of the former—what Plutarch calls Brutus's "Spartan style"—contrasting with the far more persuasive dramatic rhetoric of the latter. It will be justly argued that Shakespeare's Ovid owes much to Golding, as his Plutarch obviously derives from North. But in a culture as imbued with the classics as Elizabethan England was, that cannot be the last word. Shakespeare's version of the Venus and Adonis story is nowhere in Golding; the psychological acuity of *Julius Caesar*, *Antony and Cleopatra*, *Coriolanus*, will not be found in North's Plutarch. The refiguration of classical history and myth depended on realizing and humanizing the ancients through finding the right language for them, inventing a classical English.

Ben Jonson took more from his classical originals, and was proud of doing so. He also saw performance not as the end point of the play, but as an intermediate stage in a process eventuating in the book. Drama was a mirror of society—the Globe's motto collapsed the two, *Totus mundus agit histrionem*, the whole world is an actor, all the world's a stage—but whether the mirror offered a reflection that was accurate or distorted depended on the interests of the spectator; and of course, an accurate reflection may be too revealing, entirely too accurate. Jonson saw his true audience as readers. In this way he exercised more control over both the presentation of his work and its reception. Publication, however, had its own dangers, exemplified in Jonson's arrest over *Sejanus*, which must have been prompted by the publication of the quarto in 1605, not by the single court performance two years earlier.[17]

Jonson's programmatic classicism, his adherence to his classical sources, may have cost him a popular audience for his two tragedies, though it is not clear that the failure of *Sejanus* and *Catiline* was a response to their latinity.[18] In dedicating *Catiline* to the Earl of Pembroke Jonson says that "in these jig-given times" his play is "a legitimate poem." *Catiline* is better than *Sejanus*, Jonson says, because in it he has not made the concessions to popular taste acknowledged in the preface "To the Readers" of *Sejanus*: the lack of a proper chorus, and the failure to observe the unity of time. The fact of the dedication to Pembroke itself invokes a significant context: his mother Mary Herbert, Countess of Pembroke, was, as we have seen, at the center of a classicizing movement in closet drama, with her *Antonie* (1590/1593) and her patronage of Daniel's *Cleopatra* (1595). Presenting *Catiline* at a public playhouse may appear to have been misguided, but Inga-Stina Ewbank notes that from the 1580s onward there were several public theater plays dealing with the same period of Roman history.[19] In any case, the assumption that, at the very least, sophisticated audiences would appreciate the play was surely not unfounded: all academic drama was on the classical model, and indeed, much of it was in Latin; for educated spectators the mode would have been entirely familiar. But more to the point, critiques that undertake to blame the initial failure of *Catiline* on its uncompromising classicism need to explain its success with the next generation of playgoers. It was revived by the King's Men in the 1630s, and the title page of the second quarto, published in 1635, declares it "now acted by His Majesty's Servants with great applause." It became Jonson's most widely cited play throughout the rest of the century.[20]

The problem with the premieres of both *Sejanus* and *Catiline* may well have been not latinity but Jonson. Robert Herrick testifies to the fact that even *The Alchemist* had had its detractors:

> Such ignorance as theirs was, who once hist
> At thy unequal'd Play, the *Alchymist*:
> Oh fie upon 'em![21]

Obviously there were things to dislike about Jonson other than his classicism; the classicism was generally an object of admiration. Several of the eulogists in the memorial volume *Jonsonus Virbius* specifically praise his reform of the language of the stage, his classicized English. John Cleveland declares Jonson

> Tun'd to the *highest Key* of *ancient* Rome,
> Returning all her *Musique* with his owne.[22]

Henry King writes,

> Amongst those soaring *Wits* that did dilate
> Our *English*, and advance it to the *rate*
> And *value* it now holds, *thy selfe* was one
> Helpt lift it up to such proportion,
> That thus *refin'd* and *roab'd* it shall not spare
> With the full *Greeke* or *Latine* to compare.[23]

Though Shakespeare, Beaumont, and Fletcher are frequent points of comparison in the volume, for William Habington, the relevant poets are the ancient ones:

> Looke up! where *Seneca* and *Sophocles*,
> Quicke *Plautus*, and sharpe *Aristophanes*,
> Enlighten yon bright *Orbe*! Doth not your eye,
> Among them, one farre larger fire, descry,
> At which their lights grow pale? 'tis *Johnson*, there
> He shines your *Starre* who was your *Pilot* here.[24]

For his acolytes, Jonson was defined by his classicism; and indeed, for several of the eulogists he made English a classical language:

> Twenty ages after, men shall say
> (If the world's story reach so long a day,)
> *Pindar* and *Plautus* with their double Quire
> Have well translated Ben the English Lyre.
> What sweets were in the Greek or Latine knowne,
> A naturall metaphor has made *thine* owne:
> Their loftie language in thy Phrase so drest,
> And neat conceits in our own *tongue* exprest,
> That Ages hence, Criticks shall question make
> Whether the Greeks and Romanes English spake.[25]

Moreover,

> Thou shalt be read as *Classick Authors*; and
> As *Greeke* and *Latine* taught in every Land.[26]

The point here is not the accuracy of the perception, but the terms in which the praise is conceived. Jonson conceived his own praise of Shakespeare in the same terms, summoning

> *thund'ring* Aeschilus,
> Euripides, *and* Sophocles *to us,*
> Paccuvius, Accius, *him of* Cordova [Seneca] *dead,*
> *To life againe, to heare thy Buskin tread,*
> *And shake a Stage: Or, when thy Sockes were on,*
> *Leave thee alone, for the comparison*
> *Of all that insolent* Greece *or haughtie* Rome
> *Sent forth, or since did from their ashes come.*[27]

Jonson the classicist calls the ancient tragic poets to witness that in the creation of an English classic theater, small Latin and less Greek was quite enough Latin and Greek.

Chapter 7

Looking Backward

What Classics?

Stuart Gillespie, writing of the persistence of translations of the classics throughout English literature, argues that "the primary means of access English poets have to ancient writers *always* tends to be through the translations of previous English poets (rather than through Latin or Greek texts)" (emphasis in the original). More than this, he shows that "historical English translations have been influential on interpretation of ancient works much more widely, inflecting readings by those we might assume, and who would themselves probably expect, to be capable of more independent responses, unmediated by translations of the past."[1] This chapter examines a few selected examples of the response of later ages, for the most part to translations of Homer. As we shall see, the familiar assumption that the classics are the means of rescuing English from its rude vernacular manners continues to be visible in various permutations even up to the present day, but consensus is always incomplete because there is never any agreement for more than a generation or two about what would constitute a properly classical English.

The use of the term "the classics" to refer specifically to the literature of ancient Greece and Rome dates only from the eighteenth century. A good deal of intellectual baggage accompanied it. I begin with a zany poem called "The Purchase of Poets, or a Dialogue betwixt the Poets, and Fame, and Homers

Marriage" by Margaret Cavendish, Duchess of Newcastle, published in 1653, in which

> A Company of Poets strove to buy
> Parnassus Hill, where Fame thereon doth lye.

But poets have no money, and in any case, Fame says,

> this hill I'll neither sell nor give,
> But they that have most wit shall with me live.[2]

So the poets woo Fame with their wit. All the contestants, needless to say, are ancient; they include Homer, Ovid, Virgil, Horace, Juvenal, Catullus, Tibullus, Lucan, and a host of nameless others—Homer alone among those named is Greek. Their cases are pled by their protagonists (Ovid's champion is Pythagoras), and the group is whittled down to three, Virgil, Ovid, and Homer. Fame chooses Homer as the originary poet, the source of all subsequent poetry—a marginal gloss explains that "al Poets imitate Homer"—and marries him. The underlying assumption is, of course, that all poets are therefore inferior to Homer. Chapman had made the assumption explicit in introducing his *Iliad*: "Of all bookes extant in all kinds, Homer is the first and best."[3] Homer's priority is assured by the supposition that he imitated no one, and his eminence by the claim that no one could imitate him successfully. By Cavendish's time, the assumption was all but universal. Thomas Grantham, translating the first book of the *Iliad* in 1659, declares that "Homer he is the heart, the sun, the light of all the Poets, without him they are like dials without the Sun; like candles unlighted."[4]

Cavendish would have known Homer only in translation. She had not studied Greek (she herself says in a prefatory epistle to her *Poems and Fancies* that she knew no language other than English), so she cannot have conceived herself as a poet to be imitating Homer in any direct sense. She was, however, a prodigious reader and a serious and original philosopher, and her brother John Lucas, to whom she was close, was a classical scholar. She was enormously literate, and the idea that the only real poetry is classical, and that

Homer is the poetic benchmark (rather than Virgil or Ovid)—that, moreover, the sole model of poetry is Homer, Homer is the source of all later poetry—is worth pausing over, especially coming from her: it should be emphasized that these assumptions do not at all reflect the literary and educational practice of the England of her time. The Latin poets continued to be central; taught, admired, and translated. Cavendish's poem is jocular; but the idea that Homer is the one true classic is not only a joke, it is also a truism. In the previous century, Virgil and Ovid were the essential classics, Latin was the *lingua franca*, and Greek, as we have seen, despite its inclusion in the higher reaches of the school curriculum, was still in 1600 a trope for incomprehensibility. Homer's remoteness, his relative inaccessibility to even educated English readers, was surely part of the point for the seventeenth and eighteenth centuries. The classic grew increasingly less universal, more elitist and exclusive.

But once Homer became the quintessential classic, he also became the ideal poet, without weaknesses or imperfections. This did not happen all at once: Horace's assertion in the *Ars Poetica* that Homer was not always at his best (*indignor quandoque bonus dormitat Homerus*, "I resent it when good Homer dozes") seemed simply common sense for a millennium and a half, and was cited with approval by Dryden: "Horace acknowledges that honest Homer nods sometimes."[5] The expression "Homer nods" is generally credited to Pope in the *Essay on Criticism*—the phrase is indeed there, but Pope is denying the claim: "Those oft are Stratagems which Errors seem, / Nor is it Homer nods, but we that dream."[6] By the beginning of the eighteenth century, this was the usual attitude—how could the essential classic be anything less than perfect? A century and a half later Matthew Arnold cites the Horace passage in *On Translating Homer* and declares that it does not mean what everyone thinks it means. Arnold is presumably denying that Homer ever nods, but, characteristically elusive, he then says he is not going to discuss the matter further.[7]

The adulation of the classics, of course, also produced dissenters, a reaction against humanism by intellectuals who had been deeply trained in the humanistic disciplines. Francis Bacon in *The Advancement of Learning* declares that "These times [i.e., the present] are the ancient times, when the world is ancient, and not those which we count antient"—we ourselves are the ancients, and no reverence is due to antiquity. The past was not wiser than the present; indeed, the present is wiser because we build on the knowledge of the past.[8] Sir Thomas Browne confronted the idealization of the classics directly and with indignation. In *Pseudodoxia Epidemica* Browne deplores "a peremptory adhesion unto Authority, and more especially the establishing of our belief upon the dictates of Antiquity," which he calls "the mortallest enemy unto knowledge, and that which hath done the greatest execution upon truth." What is pernicious about this is not simply that it impedes the possibility of any skeptical empiricism of our own (knowledge of the classics, Browne insists, is not knowledge at all), but even more that there is nothing about classical writers that entitles them to be considered authoritative: "their volumes are meer collections, drawn from the mouthes or leaves of other Authors," and here we come to the real point: "Not a few transcriptively, subscribing their Names unto other mens endeavours, and meerly transcribing almost all they have written. The *Latines* transcribing the *Greeks*, the *Greeks* and *Latines* each other."[9] He then gives a compendious list of classical offenders, including many of the monuments of ancient literature, history, and science: Pliny, Lucian, Apuleius, Aristotle, Aelian, Athenaeus, "and many more," he says. And then, hitting his stride, "Even the magnified *Virgil* hath borrowed almost all his Works: his *Eclogues* from *Theocritus*, his *Georgicks* from *Hesiod* and *Aratus*, his *Aeneads* from *Homer*; the second Book thereof, containing the exploit of *Sinon* and the *Trojan Horse* (as *Macrobius* observeth) he hath *verbatim* derived from *Pisander*."[10]

Browne then moves on to the classics of his own profession, with ancient medical writers cribbing from Galen and from each other. Here is the moralization he draws from this catalogue of thievery: "And thus may we perceive the Ancients were but men, even like our selves. The practise of transcription in our dayes was no monster in theirs: *Plagiarie* had not its Nativity with Printing." And lest we argue that none of this is *really* plagiarism, since none of it involves any intention to deceive, Browne in his final revision of the *Pseudodoxia* blocks that exit too, adding this: "Nor did they only make large use of other Authors, but often without mention of their names. *Aristotle*, who seems to have borrowed many things from *Hippocrates*, in the most favourable construction, makes mention but once of him, and that by the by, and without reference unto his present Doctrine. *Virgil*, so much beholding unto *Homer*, hath not his name in all his Works; and *Plinie*, who seems to borrow many Authors out of *Dioscorides*, hath taken no notice of him. I wish men were not still content to plume themselves with others Feathers." Browne does not even allow the distinction between plagiarism and allusion, or acknowledged borrowing, to be a real one: "Fear of discovery, not single ingenuity [simple honesty] affords Quotations rather than Transcriptions." That is, the only reason people put things in quotes is not that they are honest but that they are afraid of being found out. "The ancients were but men, even like ourselves": everybody is guilty here—and one of Browne's modern editors remarks tartly, predictably, about this passage, "his comments were not very original."[11] Plagiarism is the original sin, the sin we are all guilty of. The only reason Homer is not indicted is that Browne doesn't know whom he copied from.

What Browne says is that the price of literature, the price of a written tradition, is plagiarism; without plagiarism there is no Virgil, no Ovid, no Aristotle. This is not, obviously, being offered as an argument in favor of plagiarism, but it also is not a claim, as it well might be, that plagiarism is a necessary evil, that the sin that makes us mortal also makes us human. Plagiarism is the symptom, not the disease: the attack on plagiarism becomes almost at once an attack on Virgil, Ovid, Aristotle. *That* is the disease: literature, culture, the classics, are precisely the problem. They are the stronghold of the pernicious adherence to authority, the enemy of experience and empirical science. Virgil imitated Homer because Homer was a classic, the poetry Virgil cared most about, the center of the canon; and that is what has to go: the canon, the tradition, the desire to preserve and renew the greatness of the past—in short, everything that humanism stood for.

It took several centuries for Bacon's and Browne's arguments to become guides to education, but with the assumption that the sciences have nothing to learn from the humanities, that science and engineering are the core disciplines, and that ethics, philosophy, history, and the training of the imagination are irrelevant to the world served by science and engineering, the "real" world of business and politics, their triumph is surely complete. For the sciences now to apply humanistic values to the research they pursue, to question the ethics of what their work enables governments and corporations to accomplish, is considered at best flippant, at worst treasonable.

Ogilby's Classics

John Ogilby's Virgil, Aesop, and Homer were among the most splendid books seventeenth-century England produced. Ogilby was not a classical scholar. He was born around 1600, a Scot with little formal education, though John Aubrey says he was "bred to his grammar," that is, brought up to speak and write correctly—judging from his subsequent career, he was exceptionally charming and persuasive.[12] His father was imprisoned for debt; while still young he won money in a lottery sufficient to pay off the debts and set his father free—Aubrey says it was a Virginia Company lottery, which took place in 1612. The story has been considered dubious, since Ogilby would have been only twelve at the time; but it may be an indication that he always took risks and had a precocious feel for what would pay off—certainly throughout his life he survived an astonishing number of crises, and always prospered. Moving to England in his teenage years, he initially supported himself as a dancing master. He attracted the attention of Buckingham, and is said to have danced with him in Ben Jonson's masque *The Gipsies Metamorphos'd* (1621); but an injury ended Ogilby's career as a dancer, and thereafter he used his aristocratic connections to attach himself to the household of Thomas Wentworth, later Earl of Strafford. When Wentworth was sent to Ireland as lord deputy in 1633, Ogilby accompanied him as tutor to Wentworth's children. While there, Ogilby established Ireland's first commercial theater, in Dublin. The theater was a success, but it and Ogilby's Irish career ended with the Irish rebellion of 1641 and Wentworth's recall and fall from power. Ogilby barely escaped from Ireland with his life.

But he was energetic and phenomenally inventive. Returned to England in the midst of the growing civil war, in his midforties he somehow learned enough Latin and Greek to embark on a series of classical translations. The first of these was a Virgil in 1649, initially privately marketed through the Merchant Taylors Company, of which he was a member, and offered to the public the next year. This was a hefty octavo with a handsome title page engraved by William Marshall, but otherwise unadorned. In the dedication to William Seymour, Duke of Somerset—a royalist general with a distant claim to the throne, and briefly the husband of King James's cousin Lady Arbella Stuart—Ogilby ascribes any roughness in his style to his Scottish childhood, acknowledging that the translation "may relish more of *Thrace* then *Greece*, having been bred in phlegmatick Regions, and among people returning to their ancient barbarity." If we recall Chapman and Cavendish, it is worth noting that by 1649, even in a Virgil translation, the stylistic ideal is presumed to be Greek, not Roman. Ogilby promises a more elegant volume "when time shall ripen more ornament of Sculpture and Annotations."[13] Clearly the idea of a series of splendidly produced and illustrated classics was part of the plan from the beginning.

The only previous English examples of the genre were Sir John Harington's 1591 *Orlando Furioso*, with engraved plates based on those of the Italian editions, and George Sandys's *Metamorphoses*, initially published without illustrations in 1626, and then in 1632 with full-page plates engraved after designs by Francis Cleyn (folios of the classics with woodcut illustrations, chiefly Terence, Virgil, and Ovid, had been published on the continent from the late fifteenth century). The Harington and Sandys were handsome folios, though in comparison with Ogilby's classics they seem modest. Indeed, Sandys's Ovid was reissued in 1640 in a larger format; but as soon as one opened the book, it became clear that this was not a grander edition, but merely a way of saving paper: the text was now in double column, and the illustrations were those of 1632 with wider margins. Ogilby's models were not these, but massive French editions such as Blaise de Vigenère's *Images* of Philostratus (1618) and Nicolas Renoüard's *Métamorphose* (1619), both sumptuously illustrated with engraved plates. In England, the massive folio format was used for the second Beaumont and Fletcher collection, *Fifty Comedies and Tragedies* (1679), though the only illustration was a portrait of Fletcher, reused from Humphrey Moseley's 1649 edition—Moseley had written apologetically that no portrait of Beaumont could be found. The format was used again for the 1692 Ben Jonson folio, again with only a frontispiece portrait. The first English poetry to be treated on the model offered by Ogilby's editions was Jacob Tonson's huge 1688 *Paradise Lost*, with engraved frontispieces for every book, declaring finally that Milton was a classic in the modern mode.

Throughout his life Ogilby was a committed royalist, and his majestic editions are a reflection of his politics—the dedication of the Virgil to a royalist general in 1649, by which time the cause was definitively lost, is indicative. Of course, there were aristocrats fighting on both sides in the civil war, and these books appealed to any bibliophiles with a taste for luxury, the means to afford it, and a great deal of room on their library shelves; but the political agenda was always visible. Ogilby inaugurated his series of grand illustrated classics with an Aesop in 1651, first published in quarto with illustrations by Cleyn, who had done the illustrations for Sandys's Ovid in 1632. This was sufficiently popular so that Ogilby immediately issued a folio version with Cleyn's designs reengraved. The illustrated Virgil, again with plates by Cleyn, followed in 1654. The illustrated *Iliad*, issued in 1660 at the Restoration, is dedicated to Charles II.

Francis Cleyn has largely disappeared from art history, but in his own time he was successful and greatly admired. Originally German, he had studied in Italy, and by the 1620s was working for the king of Denmark. James I and later Charles I employed him to design tapestries at Mortlake; he was also much in demand to decorate aristocratic houses—he was already part of the patronage system within which Ogilby conceived his publication of the grand English classics.

Ogilby's royalist aesthetics were not limited to the reinvention of the classics. At Charles's coronation he produced a commemorative festival book, initially a simple account of the events and ceremonies to test the market, and then, two years later, a great full-scale memento, with fold-out plates depicting in minute detail the hundreds of lavishly dressed and uniformed participants, and a double-page spread of the coronation itself, again with the participants and spectators minutely delineated.[14] For this the artists were David Loggan and Wenceslaus Hollar. Cleyn had died in 1658; Loggan specialized in engraved portraits, and was thus an appropriate illustrator for a memento celebrating the social elite, and Hollar was famous for his London views. This magnificent volume was the model for a subsequent series of English festival books, memorials of a particularly turbulent few years: Francis Sandford's account of the coronation of James II and Mary of Modena in 1687; in the next year Michael Wright's celebration of the ill-conceived embassy sent by James II to the pope; and in 1689 the coronation book of William and Mary.

Around 1661 Ogilby had become the royal printer. He lost much of his stock in the London fire of 1666, but recouped his losses through a lottery in which the prizes were selected from his remaining folios (one of the winners was Samuel Pepys, who came away with the Aesop and the Coronation volume). At the end of his career, Ogilby turned to cartography and topography. In 1671 he was appointed the royal cosmographer, and produced a series of handsome atlases. In 1675, the year before his death, he published his road atlas of Britain, *Britannia [. . .] an illustration of the kingdom of England and dominion of Wales: by a geographical and historical description of the principal roads thereof,* the work for which he is best known.

Ogilby's classics were admired in their own time; they are now bibliophiles' treasures, but they are admittedly no more than that. Thomas Hobbes, an excellent classicist who had translated Thucydides in his youth, near the end of his life produced a graceful duodecimo Homer in pentameter quatrains. In an introductory essay on heroic poetry, he asserts the superiority of Homer to all other poets, but then adds that he makes no claims for the virtues of his own translation: "Why then did I write it? Because I had nothing else to do. Why publish it? Because I thought it might take off my Adversaries from shewing their folly upon my more serious Writings, and set them upon my Verses to shew their wisdom. But why without Annotations? Because I had no hope to do it better than it is already done by Mr. *Ogilby.*"[15] This avoids saying anything about the quality of Ogilby's verse; the next generation of poets positively derided it. Dryden in *MacFlecknoe* declares Ogilby's volumes good only for wrapping pies and toilet paper, while Pope in the *Dunciad* makes him the "great forefather" of bad poetry.[16] Ogilby's translations are surely no better than serviceable, but it is fair to say that the translations were not the point. These are assertively beautiful classics, like nothing previously produced in England, and all their pretensions are in their conception and its material embodiment. Despite Dryden's contempt, his own Virgil was directly modeled on Ogilby's, even reusing Francis Cleyn's plates for the illustrations.

Blackwall's Classics

Anthony Blackwall (d. 1730) was a classical scholar, cleric, and schoolmaster, author of an edition of the works of the Greek poet Theogonis, with a translation into Latin, and of a Latin grammar for primary schools. But by far his most influential work, *An Introduction to the Classics*, became a standard school text, still being used in the nineteenth century. It is a barometer of its age, hyperbolic in its admiration for the ancients, but also fascinatingly ambivalent. It opens with many pages of praise for Greek and Roman writers, who "flourish'd in those happy Times, when *Learning* and all the *Polite Arts* were come to their Perfection and Standard,"[17] and even more for the culture that supported and encouraged literature, observing that Homer, Herodotus, Virgil, Cicero, Sallust, Horace, were all hugely admired in their own time. Juvenal is praised because, though his satires are full of vice, he disapproves of it. But—and here the ambivalence becomes clear—Ovid is cited only once, in order to assert that all the fables about gods coming to earth are actually imperfect versions of the descent of biblical angels to interact with mortals (though not, presumably, to rape, transform, and then abandon them).

How shall we reconcile the models of literature, the repository of wisdom, with the truth of Christian revelation? Suddenly Blackwall's line of argument changes: everything in the classics is a premonition or a partial account of something in the Jewish and Christian sacred scriptures. Now the glorification of Greece and Rome is implicitly recanted—suddenly, the classics are full of faults. The praise of Juvenal is abruptly withdrawn: "Here I am aware, that upon this Commendation of *Juvenal*, an objection will be made against some faulty Passages; which I am so far from being able to defend, that I think they are not fit to be mention'd. Whence we may learn, that the greatest *Beauties* in the *Pagan Morals* are mix'd with considerable *Blemishes*; that they have no System so *pure*, but some *Taint* cleaves to it." Blackwall's classical pantheon thus includes no Martial, Catullus, Propertius, Lucretius; and even the single reference to Ovid is omitted from the index. For all the glory of the classics, they are in fact dangerous: "Only the *Christian Institution* furnishes a sufficient and perfect Scheme of *Morality*."[18] Blackwall spent the last years of his life making a case for the Christian scriptures as the real classics, and hence the essential literary models. His final work, published in 1725, was *The Sacred Classics Defended and Illustrated, or, An essay humbly offered towards proving the purity, propriety, and true eloquence of the writers of the New Testament.* Here he mounted a strenuous attack on the notion—the fact, surely—that the Greek of the New Testament was not properly classical, but demotic. This argument, however quixotic, was essential if the sacred texts were to be considered true classics, models of style as well as of ethics and orthodoxy. But since the Christian scriptures consist of the Old Testament as well as the New, the study of Hebrew should have been equally essential to anyone serious about the sacred classics (as it was to Milton); but Blackwall's project was not really about defending the scriptures, it was about rendering the New Testament socially respectable, or "classy."

On Translating Homer

Chapman's transition from the Elizabethan fourteeners of his *Iliad* to the pentameter couplets of his *Odyssey* assumed that the model for Homer in English should be contemporary English poetry. Pope made the same assumption a century later, with great success for his own age—Samuel Johnson called it "the noblest version of poetry that the world has ever seen."[19] Cowper, however, near the end of the century, adopting Miltonic diction and verse for his Homer, returned to an antique and literary—or "classic"—English. By the next century, critics were objecting that Homer in English should make English sound instead like Homer's Greek—Richard Bentley, indeed, was reported to have leveled a similar criticism at Pope: "A pretty poem, Mr. Pope, but you must not call it Homer." The story is surely apocryphal, but for a scholar like Bentley any attempt by Pope at translating Homer would necessarily have been insufficiently learned. Pope felt Bentley's condescension, and included him in the *Dunciad*; Bentley's nephew Thomas, defending his uncle, declared Pope's Greek rudimentary, which was certainly not the case.[20] But the charge followed logically from the mere fact that Pope's Homer was in a modern English idiom.

Johnson's praise was tempered by his opinion that, however much Greek Pope knew, Homer is really not very difficult to translate. "Minute enquiries into the force of words are less necessary in translating Homer than other poets, because his positions are general, and his representations natural, with very little dependence on local or temporary customs, on those changeable scenes of artificial life, which, by mingling original with accidental notions, and crowding the mind with images which time effaces, produces ambiguity in diction, and obscurity in books. . . . Homer has fewer passages of doubtful meaning than any other poet either in the learned or in modern languages."[21]

Scholars of Greek would surely not agree, but the proliferation of translations throughout the eighteenth and nineteenth centuries may perhaps lend some force to the claim.

But what should English Homer sound like? In 1861 Matthew Arnold used his professorship of poetry at Oxford as a platform for entering the debate and laying down principles for translating Homer, which were also principles for rendering English poetry properly serious. The fact that the butt of his attack, the crucial bad example, was the work of a classical scholar, moved the debate away from one about accuracy to one about taste—it was not enough to construe the Greek correctly. *On Translating Homer* was prompted by the *Iliad* of Francis William Newman, published in 1856. Newman, the younger brother of John Henry Newman, was a brilliant and eccentric polymath: linguist, mathematician, dissenting missionary, enthusiastic devotee of a mass of causes. Lionel Trilling describes him:

> His philological pursuits were unremitting; besides Hebrew, Greek, Latin, Sanscrit, French, Spanish, Italian and Danish, he learned Berber, Libyan, Arabic, Abyssinian, Gothic, Chaldean, Syriac and Numidian; he translated Horace into English, *Hiawatha* into Latin and *Robinson Crusoe* into Latin and Arabic. . . . He became a militant vegetarian, an intransigeant anti-vivisectionist, an enthusiastic anti-vaccinationist. "I am anti-everything," he said in one of his rare moments of self-consciousness. He was much concerned with politics; he believed firmly in democracy but desired to "ward it off" for England. He loved "the people" but thought them lazy and shiftless, too highly paid and too much addicted to beefsteak. He was a partisan of Hungarian independence and believed that Hungary would benefit considerably from the introduction of the Bactrian camel. . . . The perfection of the soul, he said, lay in its becoming *woman.*[22]

This makes him sound ridiculous, full of contradictions and foolishness, but to his contemporaries he was not at all a figure of fun. George Eliot called him "our blessed St. Francis," Carlyle described him as "an ardently inquiring soul, . . . of sharp-cutting, restlessly advancing intellect, and the mildest pious enthusiasm."[23] In one sense, he was an easy mark, but in a deeper sense he was all but impregnable, the embodiment of everything that Arnold saw as wrong with England, but that the age admired. As Trilling says:

> The British mind, in its depths where it was aflame with spiritism, mesmerism, hydropathy and the innumerable sects of Protestantism, and on its heights where it was hot after all the modernisms of the intellect, was summed up for Arnold in Francis Newman. Faddist, populist, liberal, agnostic, eccentric, this man puts his hand to Homer. The juxtaposition is almost too pat; the opportunity cannot be missed: "The eccentricity . . . the arbitrariness, of which Mr. Newman's conception of Homer offers so signal an example, are not a peculiar failing of Mr. Newman's own; in varying degrees they are the great defect of English intellect, the great blemish of English literature."[24]

Eccentricity and arbitrariness are the besetting sins of the age; they are not a "peculiar failing" of Newman's, but "the great defect of English intellect, the great blemish of English literature." In fact, Newman's Homer is certainly eccentric, but it is also deeply English. For his prosody, doubtless without realizing it, Newman went back three centuries, to what had been "natural" in the sixteenth century. The verse is fourteeners with heavy caesuras; to anyone who has been reading Chapman's *Iliad*, Phaer's *Aeneid*, or Golding's Ovid, the only thing unusual about this Homer is that it is unrhymed.

> Of Peleus' son, Achilles, sing,   oh goddess, the resentment
> Accursed, which with countless pangs   Achaia's army wounded,
> And forward flung to Aïdes   full many a gallant spirit
> Of heroes, and their very selves   did toss to dogs that ravin,
> And unto every fowl, (for so   would Jove's device be compass'd);
> From that first day when feud arose   implacable, and parted
> The son of Atreus, prince of men   and Achileus the godlike.

Newman had produced an English version of Homeric metrics with reasonable success. Arnold's principal objection was to the translation's diction—Newman, observing that for Greeks of the classical period Homer's language was archaic, used a number of English archaisms throughout the poem. Arnold writes,

> Why are Mr. Newman's lines faulty? They are faulty, first, because, as a matter of diction, the expressions 'O gentle friend,' 'eld,' 'in sooth,' 'liefly,' 'advance,' 'man-ennobling,' 'sith,' 'any-gait,' and 'sly of foot,' are all bad; some of them worse than others, but all bad: that is, they all of them as here used excite in the scholar, their sole judge, excite, I will boldly affirm, in Professor [William Hepworth] Thompson [at Cambridge] or Professor [Benjamin] Jowett [at Oxford], a feeling totally different from that excited in them by the words of Homer which these expressions profess to render.[25]

The diction is "bad"—not a useful critical term, and the accompanying explanation does little to clarify it. Arnold the critic hedges repeatedly: he has acknowledged that any translation cannot hope to replicate the sound and movement of Homer, but it should excite the same feeling in the reader that Homeric verse excites . . . well, but in whom? In the ancient Greek reader, though Arnold admits we cannot know that—and of course, the ancient reader would have been a listener: it wouldn't have mattered in the least what feeling was excited in the literate slave who was reading Homer aloud to an audience of free Athenians in Periclean Athens. Then, Arnold says, the crucial modern readers are our greatest scholars of ancient Greek, the Regius Professors at Cambridge and Oxford. But are they necessarily good judges of English verse? Arnold does not consider the question. Yet Arnold acknowledges that poor Newman is a truly distinguished classical scholar. The only credible judge is, implicitly, not Thompson or Jowett, but Arnold himself. High seriousness is not without its element of smugness.

Arnold insists that Homer is never quaint, garrulous, prosaic, low, but always both fast and grand or noble; English versions characteristically fail in one or the other of these respects. He raises so many objections to so many translations that he was accused of maintaining that no adequate translation was possible, of assuming that Homeric language was noble precisely because it was Greek—and indeed, Chapman's and Pope's versions are faulted because they sound like the best English poetry of their respective ages. In a rebuttal, Arnold denies that the task cannot be done, and protests that he is showing how to do it; however, though he offers a multitude of bad examples, he cites only a single brief instance of success. He quotes this fragment by Edward Craven Hawtrey, a passage from Book 3 in which Helen views the Greek army:

> Clearly the rest I behold of the dark-eyed sons of Achaia;
> Known to me well are the faces of all; their names I remember;
> Two, two only remain, whom I see not among the commanders,
> Castor fleet in the car, Polydeukes brave with the cestus,
> Own dear brethren of mine,—one parent loved us as infants.
> Are they not here in the host, from the shores of loved Lacedaemon,
> Or, though they came with the rest in ships that bound through the waters,
> Dare they not enter the fight or stand in the council of Heroes,
> All for fear of the shame and the taunts my crime has awakened?
> So said she;—they long since in Earth's soft arms were reposing,
> There, in their own dear land, their Fatherland, Lacedaemon.[26]

The passage is undeniably beautiful, though it is surely to the point that it comes not from a translation of the whole poem, but is offered by Hawtrey only as a sample. Whether its nobility and speed could be maintained over the more than 15,000 lines of the *Iliad* there is no way of knowing.

A number of complete versions in hexameters took up the challenge; none met with much success. Tennyson had contempt for them, and wrote a little hexameter parody:

> These lame hexameters the strong-wing'd music of Homer!
> No—but a most burlesque barbarous experiment.
> When was a harsher sound ever heard, ye Muses, in England?
> When did a frog coarser croak upon our Helicon?
> Hexameters no worse than daring Germany gave us,
> Barbarous experiment, barbarous hexameters.[27]

Newman unwisely responded to Arnold; he in fact scores a number of points, though his prose is so prolix that they mostly get lost in detail—Arnold is by far the better debater. Newman maintains that his translation had been praised by classicists, and that Arnold's Greek was deficient.[28] In rebuttal, Arnold admits the charge, but adds, paradoxically, that he wishes he had known even less Greek. It is a debater's gambit, but Arnold nowhere makes good on it—how would being less of a scholar improve one's judgment? Trilling's masterful account of Arnold's intellectual development reveals the pessimism and insecurity underlying the commitment to principle and high seriousness, and the insecurity doubtless accounts for the arrogance, but it is a mode that has long ceased to be persuasive.

The distinguished classical scholar W. H. D. Rouse, editing Arnold's lectures and Newman's reply at the turn of the century—by which time Newman was long forgotten and Arnold all but canonized—acknowledges that Arnold's Greek simply was not good enough to support many of his contentions, but praises his critical principles. Rouse and Arnold shared many critical assumptions. Rouse writes, "[At the present time] the criterion of excellence is too often an arbitrary whim, or a taste imperfect because founded on imperfect knowledge. The modern critic has rarely studied the masters of his own art. Longinus is hardly known to him even by name; Aristotle is little more than a name; and the great masterpieces of literary style, which are nearly all Greek, are left aside as antiquated lumber."[29] Just as there is something enviable about Arnold's supreme confidence in his own judgment, so there is in Rouse's conviction of the excellence of his own taste because of his classical erudition—"imperfect taste," he tells us, is a consequence of imperfect knowledge; but knowledge is conceived entirely as knowledge of the classics. Even in Rouse's terms, such a claim is problematic: Newman was a much better classicist than Arnold, and that did nothing to rectify Newman's taste. At this distance, understanding the terms of the debate is an exercise in critical archeology. It is a very long time since the claim that not having studied Longinus disqualifies a critic could be taken seriously, or that the proper models of English style "are nearly all Greek"—one wonders what the exceptions could have been.

Homer's poetry was never "modern." Homeric Greek, all the commentators agree, was a literary dialect that was never actually spoken. Its familiarity for the Greeks of Sophocles's time is regularly compared with that of the King James Bible for us (at least, for us until a couple of generations ago). This is not an argument for translating Homer into King James Bible English; it is, on the contrary, a recognition of just how problematic an undertaking the translation of Homer is. Moreover, no translator can now assume an audience of readers who have studied Greek, for whom appreciating the translation involves comparing it with the original, and who will have their own ideas about the character of Homeric style—even Newman in 1856 says he is writing for readers with no Greek, "the unlearned public."[30] One hundred and fifty years later, it appears that Newman was more right about Homeric Greek than Arnold. Maybe the archaic words in Newman's translation that so offended Arnold are in fact a good approximation of Homeric style. Arnold himself acknowledges that "[Homer's] language was as familiar to Sophocles, we may be quite sure, as the language of the Bible is to us."[31] Rouse ups the ante considerably, adding "perhaps almost like Chaucer."[32]

What Homer Sounds Like

Until the eighteenth century, whether or not the translation sounded like Homer was largely irrelevant; the issue was how to make it sound like classical English—hence Chapman's fourteeners, Pope's heroic couplets, and Cowper's Miltonic blank verse. But what is desirable in a translation changes as the culture changes; and particularly, as Greek is no longer a part of the standard school curriculum. The essential question has always been, in varying degrees, less whether the work sounds like Homer than whether it sounds like English, and what kind of English it sounds like. Different ages will give different answers and will find different models appropriate—the Victorian *Iliad* of Lang, Leaf, and Myers, and the *Odyssey* of Butcher and Lang, the standard translations for almost a century, took as their model the prose of the King James Bible, a choice that speaks for itself. W. G. T. Barter's 1854

Iliad and Philip Stanhope Worsley's 1861 *Odyssey* were in Spenserian stanzas, which today seem simply bizarre, but both were praised when they appeared; and surely if Milton is accepted as a valid model for the English epic, so may Spenser be. An anonymous reviewer in *The Saturday Review*, while praising Worsley's verse, objects that there are places where the translation includes bits, sometimes several lines long, that are nowhere in the original.[33] This problem is doubtless the result of the choice of the stanza form, which must be filled out; but it surely will be noticeable only to a reader continually comparing the translation with the Greek—only, that is, to an expert reviewer. For comparison, Marlowe's *Hero and Leander* contains a great deal that is not in Musaeus, and certainly in most respects misrepresents Musaeus; but nobody would claim that Marlowe is therefore inferior to Musaeus—and Musaeus in the sixteenth century was considered in a class with Homer, and even, by Scaliger, superior to Homer.

What constitutes a good translation changes rapidly. Richmond Lattimore's Homer, greatly admired in my college years, now sounds garrulous—or worse: Daniel Mendelsohn describes Lattimore as "mimicking [Homer's] craggily archaic diction," and declares that the translation has been "long popular among classicists, perhaps because it practically is Greek."[34] The most highly praised translations of the past two or three decades have been those of Robert Fagles, Stephen Mitchell, and Stanley Lombardo. On the whole, their virtue is felt to be their conversational quality—exactly their distance from Homer. This is a virtue partly because it will be attractive to high school and college students; but more deeply, as Mendelsohn argues in an admiring review of the Lombardo translation, because they remake Homer along contemporary lines, in effect, participating in the continuous creation of Homer:

> There are probably too many departures from the Greek text here, and too many blatantly "contemporary" resonances, for this to become the standard Homer of university classrooms. But in a way, those departures, those ruptures with philological exactitude, may make this "Iliad" an ideal vehicle for teaching the poetic tradition that we owe to its creator—the oldest, deadest, whitest European male. In taking

the existing text of Homer as a starting point for a brand-new performance of his own, Stanley Lombardo is following in the footsteps of the company of "Homers" who assembled that text to begin with—not breaking with tradition but joining its powerful current. That his daring new "Iliad" is so specifically of and for our time reminds us—and right now it's a point worth being reminded of—that Homer's poem is for all time.[35]

Coda

What is a classic? Mary Beard gives a characteristically tart and lucid account of the origins of the term, which is much less "classical" than it is all but universally assumed to be. She begins by observing that *classicus* is always interpreted to mean "of the first class," and metaphorically, when applied to literature or art, it relates "classic" to economic, political, or social power. But, she says, Roman writers were in fact quite unclear about the definition of "the classic." The Latin adjective is very rare. For our sense of the classic, the relevant usages appear in the *Attic Nights* of Aulus Gellius: "Two passages of this long book are particularly relevant to the idea of the 'classic' and tend to upset an idea of Roman conservative literary hierarchy. In the first (Book 6, 13), Gellius is worrying about what Marcus Cato meant, three centuries earlier by the word *classicus*. He was referring only to the men of the first class, Gellius insists—but, reassuringly, he observes that people do often wonder what *classicus* actually means." As for the application of "classic" to writing, "The second passage is the famous occasion on which Aulus Gellius (for the first time, so far as we know) used the word *classicus* metaphorically to refer to literature (Book 19, 8). In the section of this discussion that is always quoted, Gellius defers to a '*classicus* or *assiduus* writer' (translated as 'authoritative,' *assiduus* is another word that comes from Roman political hierarchy)—that is, he explains, 'one who is not *proletarius*.' It looks at first sight like a fairly conclusive proof of the link between 'classic' and 'classy' writers." But, Beard continues, it is not so simple:

> For a start, this is the only time in "classical Latin" that the word *classicus* is used to refer to writing. But even more to the point, the topic at

> issue, for which the view of a *classicus* writer is sought, is a real surprise. The debate at this part of the *Attic Nights* is all about whether some Latin words can only be used in the plural, others only in the singular. *Harena* (sand), it is said, can only be used in the singular, *quadrigae* (chariot) only in the plural. So far so good. But the joke is that if this (as is implied) is the view of the *classicus* and not *proletarius* writer, then the *classicus* is wrong—both words are reliably found in both singular and plural. Our conclusion must be (as it so often is with these problematic terms) that the term *classicus* was born problematic.[1]

Indeed, throughout the sixteenth and seventeenth centuries it was not even always clear what languages should be considered classical. For any biblical student, Hebrew was as classical as Greek and Latin (and Milton would add Chaldean and Syriac); and as we have seen, for Francis Meres, Italian was classical.

By the time T. S. Eliot delivered his Presidential Address to the Virgil Society in 1944, his critical pronouncements were being treated as oracular. Entitled "What Is a Classic?," it might have been expected to settle the matter, though given the nature of the event and the character of the audience, it was understandably designed more to confirm convictions than to persuade sceptics. Eliot, in any case, begins by disarming criticism: in defining the classic, he assures us that he is not thereby precluding any alternative uses of the term; and to say that a work is not a classic, or that a culture has not produced any classics, is not to be considered a defect. "It did happen that the history of Rome was such, the character of the Latin language was such, that at a certain moment a uniquely classical poet was possible"—though lest we assume that the classic is simply historically determined, Eliot's classic does also require a good deal of hard work: "it needed that particular poet, and a lifetime of labour on the part of that poet, to make the classic out of his material."[2]

The defining characteristic of Eliot's sense of the classic is, he says, "maturity," and he goes on to distinguish "the universal classic, like Virgil, and the classic which is only such in relation to the other literature in its own language." And language is the crucial element: "an individual author—notably Shakespeare and Virgil—can do much to develop his own language: but he cannot bring that language to maturity unless the work of his predecessors has prepared it for his final touch."[3] Nothing, therefore, in any of the vernaculars makes the grade (not even Dante, though he is a crucial figure in the narrative), but neither, surprisingly, does Homer, because we inevitably see Homer through Virgil—"it is through Rome that our parentage in Greece must be traced"[4]—and because "the conflict between the Greeks and the Trojans is hardly larger in scope than a feud between one Greek city-state and a coalition of other city-states," whereas the *Aeneid* expresses "*relatedness*, between two great cultures, and, finally, of their reconciliation under an all-embracing destiny."[5] That destiny is not, of course, the one realized in the poem: "[Aeneas's] reward was hardly more than a narrow beachhead and a political marriage in a weary middle age"; but the *Aeneid* is finally the essential classic because of Dante: Virgil's "function was to lead Dante to a vision he could never himself enjoy, lead Europe towards the Christian culture which he could never know."[6] Virgil is the universal classic because he led Dante—though more accurately, surely, Dante led him—to Christianity; or to put it more mundanely, because in the Middle Ages the *Aeneid* could be accommodated to Roman Catholic doctrine. As for that large percentage of the world that does not share Eliot's far from universal religious faith but nevertheless feels entitled to classics in such classical languages as Sanskrit and Chinese, they have to make the best of it: despite the initial disclaimer about alternative senses of the classic, Eliot assures us that Europe is "the organism out of which any greater world harmony must develop."[7]

Eliot's characteristic gravitas precludes any questions, but we may feel that the concept of the classic has here become more exclusive than capacious, or has even been refined out of existence: the only genuine classic is not even Virgil's *Aeneid*, but the *Aeneid* via Dante, Virgil foretelling Catholic Europe (I wonder how many classicists in the Virgil Society audience raised eyebrows). As to why in that case Dante is not the essential classic, the answer is that he writes in the vernacular, and Latin was the universal European language, not Italian; but put in that way, the pronouncement sounds a good deal less oracular. There is no reason to treat this as any more authoritative than the Duchess of Newcastle's declaration that Homer was the only poet chosen by Fame; and Margaret Cavendish knew she was not being serious. But Eliot was as serenely confident that his convictions constituted a historical fact as Matthew Arnold had been.

Broader definitions, however, have their own problems. Italo Calvino, in *Why Read the Classics?*, treats the question with a good deal of irony. A classic is initially defined as a book "about which you usually hear people saying: 'I'm rereading', never 'I'm reading,'" a book that people feel they ought to have read and feel guilty about not having read.[8] This suggests that for anyone purporting to be cultured, there are a large number of classics. Calvino talks most about the *Odyssey*; but his list of classics is exceedingly generous, seemingly with room for anything one fancies: "Lucretius, Lucian, Montaigne, Erasmus, Quevedo, Marlowe, the *Discourse on Method*, Goethe's *Wilhelm Meister*, Coleridge, Ruskin, Proust and Valéry, with the occasional sortie into Murasaki or the Icelandic Sagas."[9] Lucian, Ruskin, Lady Murasaki—heavens! Elsewhere in the essay Dickens and Leopardi figure significantly, but there is not a word about Virgil or Dante. We are a world away from the austere Eliot.

But Calvino makes a striking observation about the *Odyssey*: that unlike the *Iliad*, it is written as a story already known, continually being recovered—Telemachus goes off to learn it, Odysseus is constantly in danger of forgetting it. It is already a classic.[10] And perhaps that is the character of the works that form this history: the culture adopts them, translates them, continually refigures them, because they are already part of the national memory. They are not only the stories that are always reread, but also always rewritten.

Notes

CHAPTER 1

1. *Tamia* is literally a housekeeper or female steward, hence the dispenser of the household treasures, and by metonymy the treasury itself. The book is a collection of literary commonplaces. The *Comparative Discourse of Our English Poets with the Greeke, Latine, and Italian Poets* appears well into the volume, beginning on fol. 279 (of 333). The fact that Meres's comparison set includes Italy is notable—Italian for Meres is a classical language (it is, in fact, technically a dialect of Latin). His list of Italian poets is "Dante, Boccace, Petrarch, Tasso, Celiano, and Ariosto." The unexpected Celiano is the pseudonym of the Genoese poet Angelo Grillo (1557–1629), a close friend of Tasso's, and the author of madrigal lyrics set by Monteverdi, Marenzio, and others. His only known, very dubious, connection with Elizabethan literature is the claim, on the title page of Robert Chester's *Love's Martyr* (1602), to include a translation of a work of "Torquato Caeliano." The name appears to be a conflation with Tasso; no Italian source for *Love's Martyr* is known, nor has Robert Chester ever been satisfactorily identified (Shakespeare's *Phoenix and the Turtle* is also in the volume). The English poets cited as comparable with the Italians have survived much less well than their Italian counterparts: "Matthew Roydon, Thomas Atchelow [Achelley], Thomas Watson, Thomas Kid [Kyd], Robert Greene, and George Peele." In *Elizabethan Critical Essays*, edited by G. Gregory Smith, 2 vols. (Oxford: Oxford University Press, 1904, and many later reprintings), 2:319.

2. For an excellent overview, see Rita Copeland, ed., *The Oxford History of Classical Reception in English Literature, Volume 1* (Oxford: Oxford University Press, 2016), chaps. 1 and 2.

3. "Classic" and "classical" applied to literature, denoting both Greek and Roman writings and standards of excellence, had come into English by the mid-sixteenth century. The limitation of the expression "the classics" to ancient literature dates only from the eighteenth century (see Chapter 7). The *OED*'s first citation for "classical" in relation to music is from 1829, but in a context that clearly implies that the term was already in use.

4. Philip Sidney, *An Apologie for Poetrie* (1595), in Smith, *Elizabethan Critical Essays*, 1:196. (The same essay was published under the title *The Defence of Poesie*, also in 1595.)

5. Philip Sidney, Sonnet 15, line 7, in *The Poems of Sir Philip Sidney*, ed. William A. Ringler (Oxford: Clarendon Press, 1962), p. 172.

6. David Norbrook, *Writing the English Republic: Poetry, Rhetoric and Politics, 1627–1660* (Cambridge: Cambridge University Press, 1999), chaps. 1 and 5.

7. For the counterarguments, see Stuart Gillespie, *English Translation and Classical Reception* (Chichester: Wiley-Blackwell, 2011), 30; and Robert Cummings, "Translation and Literary Innovation," in *The Oxford History of Literary Translation in English*, vol. 2, *1550–1660*, ed. Gordon Braden, Robert Cummings, and Stuart Gillespie (Oxford: Oxford University Press, 2010), 32–44.

8. Cummings, "Translation," in *Oxford History of Literary Translation*, 2:42–43.

9. William Webbe, *A Discourse of English Poetry* (1586), ed. Sonia Hernández-Santano (Cambridge: Modern Humanities Research Association, 2016), 122.

10. Sidney, *Apologie*, in Smith, *Elizabethan Critical Essays*, 1:204–5. For an excellent account of the attempts at domesticating quantitative meters, see Derek Attridge, *Well-Weighed Syllables: Elizabethan Verse in Classical Metres* (Cambridge: Cambridge University Press, 1974), 109–11.

11. Richard Tottel, preface to *Songes and Sonettes Written By the Ryght Honorable Lord Henry Howard, late Earle of Surrey, and other* [Tottel's Miscellany] (London, 1557), sig. A1[v].

12. James Simpson, "The *Aeneid* Translations of Henry Howard, Earl of Surrey," in *The Oxford History of Classical Reception in English Literature*, vol. 1, *800–1558*, ed. Rita Copeland (Oxford: Oxford University Press, 2015), chap. 28.

13. Stephen Medcalf, "Classical Authors," in *The Oxford History of Literary Translation in English*, vol. 1, *To 1550*, ed. Roger Ellis (Oxford: Oxford University Press, 2008), 364.

14. See S. Gillespie, *English Translation*, 5–6.

15. Rita Copeland, "Introduction: England and the Classics from the Early Middle Ages to Early Humanism," in *Oxford History of Classical Reception*, 1:4.

16. Stuart Gillespie, "Statius in English, 1648–1747," *Translation and Literature* 8, no. 2 (1999): 157.

17. Eustache Deschamps, Ballade 285, line 10, in Eustache Deschamps, *Œuvres complètes*, ed. A. H. E. de Queux de Saint-Hilaire and G. Raynaud, 11 vols. (Paris: Firmin Didot, 1878–1903), vol. 2, p. 138.

18. David Carlson, "The Writings of Bernard André," *Renaissance Studies* 12, no. 2 (June 1998): 229–50.

19. Abraham Fleming, trans., *The Bucolics of Publius Virgilius Maro* [. . .] *Together with his Georgiks* (London, 1589), sig. A4[v].

20. For a full discussion, see Stephen Orgel, "Measuring Verse, Measuring Value in English Renaissance Poetry," in *Authority, Innovation and Early Modern Epistemology*, ed. Martin McLaughlin, Ingrid D. Rowland, and Elisabetta Tarantino (Leeds: Legenda, 2015), 97–103.

21. Only the second of the Horace translations survives. The Martial poem is *Epigrammata* 10.47, STC (2nd ed.) 17495; the Horace *Satires* 1.2, STC (2nd ed.) 13805.5.

22. Gavin Douglas, preface to *The xiii Bukes of Eneados*[. . .], trans. Gavin Douglas (London, 1553), sig. B1[r,v].

23. Kirsty Milne, "The Forgotten Greek Books of Elizabethan England," *Literature Compass* 4, no. 3 (2007): 678.

24. Milne, "Forgotten Greek Books," 678. The prose translation of *Iphigenia in Aulis* in 1553 by Jane, Lady Lumley, would have been done from a continental edition—English libraries, obviously, were not limited to books printed in England. Ivan Lupić has brilliantly charted the fortunes of *Hecuba*, the most widely known of Euripides's plays in the European Renaissance, for the most part via the Latin translation by Erasmus, but with a performance, in the Croatian verse translation by Marin Drzić, in Dubrovnik in 1559, the earliest recorded vernacular performance. Most discussions focus on the play's brief appearance in the Player's Speech in *Hamlet*, but that was a very late response to a widely circulated text. It should be added that in Shakespeare's age,

English was quite as obscure and marginal a language as Croatian, and a good deal more obscure than Greek. See Ivan Lupić, "The Mobile Queen: Observing Hecuba in Renaissance Europe," *Renaissance Drama* 46, no. 1 (2018): 25–56.

25. For a survey of early publishing and book circulation at the universities, see James Willoughby, "Universities, Colleges and Chantries," in *A Companion to the Early Printed Book in Britain, 1476–1558*, ed. Vincent Gillespie and Susan Powell (Cambridge: D. S. Brewer, 2014), 207–24.

26. In 1934 F. M. Padelford published a facsimile of the work ascribing it to the poet, but offered no real evidence; the claim was from the first considered dubious, and the translation is not now considered to be by Spenser.

27. *Plato his Apology of Socrates, and Phædo, or, Dialogue concerning the immortality of mans soul, and manner of Socrates his death carefully translated from the Greek, and illustrated by reflections upon both the Athenian laws, and ancient rites and traditions concerning the soul, therein mentioned* (London, 1675). Donald Wing, comp., *Short-Title Catalogue of Books Printed in England, Scotland, Ireland, Wales, and British America, and of English Books Printed in Other Countries, 1641–1700* [STC], 2nd ed. (New York: Modern Language Assocciation of America, 1972), P2405.

28. Willoughby, "Universities," 210.

29. The Herodotus has been very dubiously ascribed to Barnabe Riche (because the prefatory epistle is signed B. R.), but there is no evidence that Riche knew Greek, and the translation does not appear to be indebted to the only contemporary vernacular version in French.

30. A digitalization with a transcription can be found at http://images.library.yale.edu/oedipusmanuscript/oedipus/manuscript.asp, accessed 05/12/2020.

31. Gascoigne gives no acknowledgment to Surrey, but it seems likely that he knew the Virgil translations. However, this may be a case (like that of Marlowe) where blank verse was reinvented. Gascoigne says that he is writing without rhyme so that reason may rule—the alternatives "rhyme or reason" were proverbial (the earliest citations are from the mid-fifteenth century). It is also relevant that the volume is set not in black letter but entirely in roman and italic, unusual for the period, but clearly a way of classicizing the work. The accompanying *Complaint of Philomene*, however, is not in blank verse but in traditional poulter's measure. Both poems are set in italic, with the introductory material in roman.

32. [Edward Howard], *Spencer Redivivus* [. . .] *By a Person of Quality* (London, 1687). The author is now presumed to be Edward Howard; see Leicester Bradner, "The Authorship of *Spenser Redivivus*," *Review of English Studies* 14 (1938): 323–26.

CHAPTER 2

1. How exactly that happened is not clear. Marlowe's poetry must have circulated in manuscript both before and after his death in 1593, but the only evidence that it did is the fact that John Wolfe registered *Hero and Leander* and the Lucan translation for publication 1593 (but did not publish them), and in 1598, 1599, and 1600 there were manuscripts to publish. A couplet from the Ovid translations appears in Nashe's *Unfortunate Traveler* (1594)—Nashe was a close friend and admirer—but otherwise nobody quoted the poems until after they were in print. The situation is similar to that of Shakespeare's sonnets, which Meres says were circulating among Shakespeare's "private friends" in 1598, but the only evidence that this is correct is the inclusion of versions of two of them in print in *The Passionate Pilgrim* in 1599. Other than these, none

of the sonnets are quoted or appear in commonplace books until after their publication in the 1609 quarto.

2. Or maybe not. For the history of ascriptions of the authorship of *Tamburlaine* see András Kiséry, "An Author and a Bookshop: Publishing Marlowe's Remains at the Black Bear," *Philological Quarterly* 91, no. 3 (Summer 2012): 361–92. Greene's accusation of atheism against *Tamburlaine* is in *Perimedes the Blacksmith*, and includes a bit about "mad and scoffing poets . . . bred of *Merlins* race." Park Honan proposes that Merlin may be a reference to Marlowe, whose name in the Cambridge records is variously Merlinge, Marlen, Marlin. See Park Honan, *Christopher Marlowe, Poet and Spy* (Oxford: Oxford University Press, 2005), 90, 184. Harvey's poem "Gorgon, or the wonderfull yeare," written in September 1593, among a catalogue of international prodigies, may be referring to Marlowe's death with the lines "The fatall yeare of yeares is *Ninety-Three* / . . . / Weepe Powles [St. Paul's, where the booksellers were], thy Tamburlaine voutsafes to dye." The poem continues, "The graund Dissease disdain'd his toade Conceit, / And smiling at his tamberlaine contempt, / Sternely struck-home the peremptory stroke. / He that nor feared God, nor dreaded Div'll, / Nor ought admired, but his wondrous selfe." The death described, however, is by plague, and in 1593 booksellers would have had nothing to sell with Marlowe's name on it—if "thy Tamburlaine" is Marlowe, he would have been a customer, not a provider of commodities. But a notorious London braggart named Peter Shakerley, who died of plague in 1593, is mentioned several lines later, and the Tamburlaine allusion seems more likely to refer to him.

3. A facsimile and transcription of Baines's testimony are in A. D. Wright, *In Search of Christopher Marlowe* (New York: Vanguard Press, 1965), 308–9. The best biographies are those of David Riggs, *The World of Christopher Marlowe* (New York: Henry Holt, 2004), which is especially good on the works, and Park Honan, cited above.

4. For a shrewd analysis of the charges, see Jonathan Goldberg, "Sodomy and Society: The Case of Christopher Marlowe," in *Staging the Renaissance*, ed. David Scott Kastan and Peter Stallybrass (New York: Routledge, 1991), 75–82.

5. Quotations are from *Christopher Marlowe: The Complete Poems and Translations*, ed. Stephen Orgel (New York: Penguin Books, 2007); this section is adapted from my introduction to the volume.

6. See David Halperin, *One Hundred Years of Homosexuality* (New York: Routledge, 1990), 134.

7. See Patrick Cheney, *Marlowe's Counterfeit Profession* (Toronto: University of Toronto Press, 1997).

8. Thomas Beard, "Of Epicures and Atheists," in *The Theatre of Gods Judgements* (1597), 147.

9. Francis Meres, *Palladis Tamia: Wits Treasury* [. . .] (1598), sigs. 286v–7r.

10. Charles Nicholl, *The Reckoning: The Murder of Christopher Marlowe* (London: Cape, 1992), 68.

11. Cited in Tucker Brooke, *The Works of Christopher Marlowe* (Oxford: Clarendon Press, 1910), 114.

12. Spenser's summary of *The Faerie Queene* in a letter to Sir Walter Ralegh was published as an addendum to the first edition of the first three books, *The Faerie Queene. Disposed into twelve books, Fashioning XII. Morall vertues* (London, 1590). The passage cited is on page 592.

13. *The Cambridge Edition of the Works of Ben Jonson*, ed. David M. Bevington, Martin Butler, and Ian Donaldson, 7 vols. (Cambridge: Cambridge University Press, 2012), 7:559, lines 1281–82.

14. Richard Stanyhurst, "From the Dedication and Preface to the Translation of the *Aeneid*," in *Elizabethan Critical Essays*, ed. G. Gregory Smith, 2 vols. (Oxford: Oxford University Press, 1904), 1:136.

15. Desiderius Erasmus, *De Ratione Studii*, trans. W. H. Woodward (Cambridge: Cambridge University Press, 1904), 528b–530a. For a striking example of humanist education in action in the teaching of this eclogue, see Stephen Orgel, *The Reader in the Book* (Oxford: Oxford University Press, 2015), 30–35.

16. Michel de Montaigne, "De l'institution des enfans," 1.26; Michel de Montaigne, *Essayes*, trans. John Florio (London, 1613), 71. The honeybee/theft conceit for the rectification and enrichment of the language is common throughout the work of the Pléiade. Castiglione also uses it in *Il Cortegiano* for the development of grace through the imitation of graceful exemplars, though in Castiglione the bee merely "gathers," it is the courtier who "robs"; in Sir Thomas Hoby's Elizabethan translation, "even as the bee in the greene medowes fleeth allwayes aboute the grasse chousynge out flowres: So shall our Courtyer steale thys grace from them that to hys seming have it." Baldessar Castiglione, *Il Libro del Cortegiano*, ed. Giulio Preti (Torino: Einaudi, 1965), 47; *The Courtyer of Count Baldessar Castilio* (London, 1561), sig. e2r.

17. Thomas More, *The Latin Epigrams*, ed. Leicester Bradner and Charles Arthur Lynch (Chicago: University of Chicago Press, 1953), no. 220.

18. Thomas More, *The Complete Works of St. Thomas More*, vol. 8, *The Confutation of Tyndale's Answer, Book 2*, ed. Louis A. Schuster (New Haven: Yale University Press, 1973), part 1, 179 lines 10–16.

19. Thomas Phaer, *The seuen first bookes of the Eneidos* [. . .] (London, 1558), sig. x2r.

20. Philemon Holland, trans., *The Historie of the World: Commonly called The Naturall Historie of C. Plinius Secundus* (London, 1601), preface to the reader, [iv] (the prefatory matter has neither signatures nor page numbers).

21. John Brende, trans., *The Actes of the Greate Alexander* (London, 1553). References are to signature numbers in the first edition, published by Richard Tottel in 1553.

22. *Julius Cesars commentaryes, newly translatyd owte of laten in to englysshe, as much as co[n] cernyth thys realm of England sumtyme callyd Brytayne: whych is the eld'yst hystoryer of all other that can be found, that euer wrote of thys realme of England* (London, 1530). The translation was in fact based not on the Latin but on a French version.

23. *The eyght bookes of Caius Iulius Cæsar* [. . .] *translated oute of latin into English by Arthur Goldinge G[ent]* (London, 1565).

24. Golding, L. T., *An Elizabethan Puritan: Arthur Golding* (New York: Richard R. Smith, 1937), 57.

25. *Le Tragedie di M. Lodovico Dolce* [. . .] (Venice, 1566), sig. A2r.

26. See Thalia Papadopoulou, *Euripides: Phoenician Women* (London: Duckworth, 2008), 118.

27. E. W. Talbert, "Current Scholarly Works and the Erudition of Jonson's *Masque of Augurs*," *Studies in Philology* 44 (1947): 605–24; and see also Talbert's earlier article "New Light on Ben Jonson's Workmanship," *Studies in Philology* 40 (1943): 154–85. The argument was called to account by Percy Simpson in *Ben Jonson*, vol. 10, *Play Commentary, Masque Commentary*, ed. C. H. Herford, Percy Simpson, and Evelyn Simpson (Oxford: Clarendon Press, 1950), 640. Talbert implicitly recants in D. T. Starnes and E. W. Talbert, *Classical Myth and Legend in Renaissance Dictionaries* (Chapel Hill: University of North Carolina Press, 1955), 212; but see the amusingly self-defensive piece of scholarly gobbledygook on 432n69.

CHAPTER 3

1. Christopher Marlowe, *Certaine of Ovids Elegies* (Middleburgh, 1599), Elegy 1.15; Ben Jonson, *Poetaster* (London, 1602), 1.1.37–78. Jonson's version is not identical to that published in 1599; the numerous small differences render the poem smoother, and occasionally correct the metrics; it looks like a more polished draft. The poem as it appears in *Poetaster* may certainly be Jonson improving Marlowe; but it may instead derive from a Marlowe manuscript superior to that used in the 1599 volume, much of which looks like a rough draft. Both versions (the latter titled "The same by B. I.") were published together in 1603 in *All Ovids Elegies 3 Bookes* (STC [2nd ed.] 18931 and 18931a)—*Poetaster* was published in 1602.

2. Roger Ascham, *The Scholemaster* (1571), sigs. h3^{v}–h4^{r}.

3. Gabriel Harvey to Edmund Spenser, A Gallant Familiar Letter [. . .] (from Three Proper and Wittie Familiar Letters [. . .], 1580), in *Elizabethan Critical Essays*, ed. G. Gregory Smith, 2 vols. (Oxford: Oxford University Press, 1904, and many later reprintings), 1:102.

4. Harvey to Spenser, Gallant Familiar Letter, in Smith, *Elizabethan Critical Essays*, 1:105.

5. Thomas Campion, *Observations in the Art of English Poesie* (1602), in Smith, *Elizabethan Critical Essays*, 2:351–52.

6. Julius Caesar Scaliger, *Poetices Libri Septem* (Lyons: Antoine Vincent, 1561), 83, and cf. also pp. v and 113.

7. Harvey to Spenser, Gallant Familiar Letter, in Smith, *Elizabethan Critical Essays*, 1:121.

8. John Hall, *Virgidemiarum* (London, 1599), book 2, satyre 3, p. 31.

9. Robert Greene, *Menaphon: Camillas alarum to slumbering Euphues*, Preface to the Gentlemen Students [by Thomas Nashe] (1589), sig. A1^{r}; and Thomas Nashe, *The apologie of Pierce Pennilesse* (1593), sig. G3^{r}.

10. Greene, *Menaphon* (1589), sig. A1^{r}.

11. Nashe, *Apologie of Pierce Pennilesse* (1593), sig. G3^{r}. Nashe's critique had a long reach. When the book was rediscovered in the nineteenth century and reprinted in an edition of fifty copies (Edinburgh, 1836), the editor John Maidment, citing the authority of Robert Southey ("our greatest living poet"), repeats all of Nashe's strictures.

12. Hall, *Virgidemiarum* (1599), book 1, satire 6, pp. 13–14.

13. Richard Stanyhurst, "From the Dedication and Preface to the Translation of the *Aeneid*" (1582), in Smith, *Elizabethan Critical Essays*, 1:142.

14. Edmund Spenser, *The Faerie Queene* IV.ii.32. Stanyhurst's claims for the purity of the language of the Anglo-Irish are found in the *Description of Ireland* that he contributed to Holinshed's *Chronicles* (1577), 3. The best account of Stanyhurst and the implications of his prosody is in Sheldon Brammall, *The English "Aeneid"* (Edinburgh: Edinburgh University Press, 2015), chapter 1.

15. Richard Stanyhurst, trans., *Thee First Foure Bookes of Virgil His Aeneis* [. . .] (Leiden, 1582), sig. A2^{r-v}.

16. Francis Meres, *Palladis Tamia: Wits Treasury* [. . .] (1598), fol. 279^{r-v}.

17. Campion, *Observations in the Art of English Poesie*, in Smith, *Elizabethan Critical Essays*, 2:327.

18. Campion, *Observations*, in Smith, *Elizabethan Critical Essays*, 2:329.

19. Campion, *Observations*, in Smith, *Elizabethan Critical Essays*, 2:331.

20. Campion, *Observations*, in Smith, *Elizabethan Critical Essays*, 2:332.

21. Thomas Campion, *Campion's Works*, ed. Percival Vivian (Oxford: Oxford University Press, 1909), lx–lxiii.

22. Samuel Daniel, *A Defence of Ryme*, in Smith, *Elizabethan Critical Essays*, 2:359–60.

23. George Gascoigne, *Certayne Notes of Instruction*, in Smith, *Elizabethan Critical Essays*, 1:49.

24. For example, the rule that in anapestic hexameter, a spondee may be substituted for the anapest in any except the penultimate foot (that is, the penultimate foot in a hexameter line must be an anapest) is violated by Virgil about 10 percent of the time.

CHAPTER 4

1. For a plethora of examples in color, google "Classical statues painted."

2. For color photos of the pediment, google "Philadelphia Art Museum pediment" and click on Images.

3. Henry Peacham, *The Compleat Gentleman* (London, 1634), 110–12—from a section on Antiquities, not in the editions of 1622 and 1627.

4. Peter Paul Rubens, *The Letters of Peter Paul Rubens*, ed. R. S. Magurn (Cambridge, MA: Harvard University Press, 1955), 320–21.

5. The collection eventually went to the University of Oxford. Many of the sculptures are illustrated in Humphrey Prideaux, *Marmora Oxoniensia, ex Arundellianis* [. . .] (Oxford, 1676); see especially 77, 82–83.

6. Roberto Calasso, *Le nozze di Cadmo e Armonia* (Milan: Adelphi, 1988), in English translated by Tim Parks as *The Marriage of Cadmus and Harmony* (New York: Alfred A. Knopf, 1993).

7. Private communication (thank you!).

8. The painting seems to be a Jacobean copy of a Scrots original, possibly made for the Arundels as they created a gallery of the earl's ancestors. Roy Strong, in his catalogue of Tudor and Jacobean portraits, observing that the earliest reference to the work calls it a "table" (i.e., a panel painting), and that all existing versions are on canvas, concludes that the original is lost and this is a later copy. See Roy Strong, *Tudor and Jacobean Portraits* (London: H.M. Stationery Office, 1969), 1:308. Moreover, the shape of the heraldic shields is anachronistic for the 1540s, but would be appropriate for the early seventeenth century. See Rodney Dennys, *Heraldry and the Heralds* (London: Jonathan Cape, 1982), 129, 201–2. To complicate matters further, Susan James proposes that the painting did not originally depict Surrey at all, but was altered later to represent him. See Susan James, "Edward Seymour, Duke of Somerset? Re-Examining a Tudor Portrait," *British Art Journal* 2, no. 2 (2000): 14–21.

9. The roman typeface was derived from the scribal Carolingian minuscule, and was called "littera antiqua" because it was believed (incorrectly) to have been the script used by the ancient Romans.

10. Richard Haydocke, preface to *A Tracte containing the Artes of curious Paintinge, Carvinge & Buildinge* [translation of Paolo Lomazzo, *Trattato dell'arte della pittura scultura ed architettura* (Milan, 1584)](Oxford, 1598), sig. ¶5^{v}.

11. David Howarth, *Lord Arundel and His Circle* (New Haven: Yale University Press, 1985), 21.

12. Roy Strong, *Henry Prince of Wales and England's Lost Renaissance* (London: Thames and Hudson, 1986), 188.

13. Also called *Tityus Chained to the Rock*.

14. For a detailed account of Henry's collection see Strong, *Henry Prince of Wales*.

15. Howarth, *Arundel*, 69.

16. See Oliver Millar, *The Queen's Pictures* (New York: Macmillan, 1977), 40–42.

17. DNB under Howard, Thomas, fourteenth Earl of Arundel.

18. In Jonson's text he is a Dwarf Post, but Jones's drawing is labled on its mount "Dutch Post." There is, of course, no way of knowing when that was done or by whom, but the role cannot have been intended for the famous court dwarf Jeffrey Hudson, who appears in the masque a moment or so later, identified as "the queen's dwarf." There was another dwarf at court, the miniature painter Richard Gibson, and Callot's original is certainly a dwarf; but it is possible that the role was redefined in the course of production.

19. See Chapter 3, section "The Debate over Quantity." Julius Caesar Scaliger, *Poetices Libri Septem* (Lyons: Antoine Vincent, 1561), 83, and cf. also pp. v and 113.

20. Howarth, *Arundel*, 108–9.

21. The drawing is signed "Henricus Peacham" with a date that has been interpreted as 1595, or more likely, 1604, 1614, or 1615. See Jonathan Bate, ed., *Titus Andronicus*, The Arden Shakespeare (London: Routledge, 1995), 38–41.

CHAPTER 5

1. A. R. Braunmuller, "Accounting for Absence: The Transcription of Space," in *New Ways of Looking at Old Texts: Papers of the Renaissance English Text Society, 1985–1991*, ed. W. Speed Hill (Binghamton, NY: Medieval and Renaissance Texts and Studies, 1993), 47–56.

2. Mark Bland, "The Appearance of the Text in Early Modern England," *Text* 11 (1998): 94.

3. For the development in Britain, see Martha Driver, "Ideas of Order: Wynkyn de Worde and the Title Page," in *Texts and Their Contexts: Papers from the Early Book Society*, ed. John Scattergood and Julia Boffey (Dublin: Four Courts Press, 1997), 87–149.

4. A. Hyatt Mayor, *Prints and People: A Social History of Printed Pictures* (New York: Metropolitan Museum of Art, 1971), 144.

5. Mayor, *Prints and People*, 144.

6. E.g., *Grammatices primae partis liber primus Roberti W.L.L. nuperrime recognitus*, STC (2nd ed.) 25486.7, and elsewhere—in other volumes of the grammar, Pynson used a simpler purely decorative border.

7. STC (2nd ed.) 20836.

8. A similar cartouche showing Henry surrounded by councillors and courtiers (without the cherubs and the wine barrel) was used for the title page of the Great Bible, 1541.

9. *The auncient historie and onely trewe and syncere cronicle of the warres betwixte the Grecians and the Troyans* [. . .], STC (2nd ed.) 5580.

10. Jonson's involvement in the design of the frontispiece is evident; but Susanna Berger raises important methodological issues about the authority behind pictorial frontispieces, and in what sense any pictorial element related to a text can be said to be collaborative. See Susanna Berger, "Meaning and Understanding in Intellectual History," *Global Intellectual History* 5, no. 3 (May 2020): 329–54, https://doi.org/10.1080/23801883.2020.1729463.

11. In a very well argued and largely persuasive essay, Davitt Moroney argues that in fact there was a connection, via Norfolk and Cambridge, between all but one of the authors of the books with this title page, and that the connection would have been known to the publishers. The exception, however, is Sidney, and Matthew Lownes's 1605 *Arcadia*; the argument does not work out as neatly as one would like it to do. The connection, of course, would not have been evident to outsiders, who would have constituted most purchasers and readers—the question of

how readers read title pages remains unanswered. See Davitt Moroney, "Thomas Morley Portrayed," forthcoming (since 2014).

12. Steven Galbraith, "Edmund Spenser and the History of the Book, 1569–1679" (PhD diss., Ohio State University, 2006), 107.

13. Bland, "The Appearance of the Text," 99.

14. Zachary Lesser, "Typographic Nostalgia: Play-Reading, Popularity, and the Meanings of Black Letter," in *The Book of the Play*, ed. Marta Straznicky (Amherst: University of Massachusetts Press, 2006), 99–127.

15. Sabrina Alcorn Baron, "Red Ink and Black Letter: Reading Early Modern Authority," in *The Reader Revealed*, ed. Sabrina Alcorn Baron (Washington, DC: Folger Shakespeare Library, 2001), 24.

16. Baron, "Red Ink and Black Letter," 23.

17. See Daniel Wakelin, "Humanism and Printing," in *A Companion to the Early Printed Book in Britain, 1476–1558*, ed. Vincent Gillespie and Susan Powell (Cambridge: D. S. Brewer, 2014), 241.

18. Arthur Marotti, *Manuscript, Print, and the English Renaissance Lyric* (Ithaca: Cornell University Press, 1995), 283.

19. Stephen Orgel, "Textual Icons: Reading Early Modern Illustrations," in *Spectacular Performances* (Manchester: Manchester University Press, 2011), 180–87. This adds some material to David Carlson, "Woodcut Illustrations of the Canterbury Tales, 1483–1602," *The Library*, 6th ser., 19 (1997): 25–67.

20. Martha Driver, "Woodcuts and Decorative Techniques," in *A Companion to the Early Printed Book in Britain, 1476–1558*, ed. Vincent Gillespie and Susan Powell (Cambridge: D. S. Brewer, 2014), 95–123.

21. What is being corrected? Are these Shakespeare's mistakes, or the mistakes of the scribe who prepared the play for the press, or those of the first compositor incorrectly reading a correct manuscript? Or are the mistakes perfectly correct, and is the point that Holofernes's Latin is at fault?

CHAPTER 6

1. Caxton appended it to the English translation of Cicero's *De Senectute*, STC (2nd ed.) 5293.

2. Greg Walker, *The Politics of Performance in Early Renaissance Drama* (Cambridge: Cambridge University Press, 1998), 10.

3. Similarly, the prefatory note to Shakespeare's *Rape of Lucrece* gets the concluding action wrong. If Medwall's and Shakespeare's misrepresentations were deliberate, there seems (as I have suggested) to be a point to Medwall's; but there cannot be a similar explanation for Shakespeare's. Did someone else write the prefatory note to *The Rape of Lucrece* and read the poem carelessly? Did Shakespeare simply forget the details of the plot?

4. Daniel Wakelin, *Humanism, Reading, and English Literature, 1430–1530* (Oxford: Oxford University Press, 2007), 163–64.

5. Clare Wright, "Henry Medwall, *Fulgens and Lucres*," in *The Oxford Handbook of Tudor Drama*, ed. Thomas Betteridge and Greg Walker (Oxford: Oxford University Press, 2012), 185.

6. The exception is *Gorboduc*, which is marketed as a play by two aristocrats, performed before the queen.

7. The translation is by Dana Sutton, in *William Gager: The Complete Works* (London: Routledge, 2019), 1:2.

8. For two excellent overviews, see Russ McDonald, "Jonsonian Comedy and the Value of *Sejanus*," *Studies in English Literature* 21, no. 2 (1981): 287–305; and John G. Sweeney III, "*Sejanus* and the People's Beastly Rage," *ELH* 48, no. 1 (Spring 1981): 61–82.

9. John Beaulieu to Sir Thomas Puckering, January 10, 1632/3. Thomas Birch, comp., *The Court and Times of Charles the First*, 2 vols. (London, 1848), 2:216.

10. British Library, Add. MS 480, fol. 359v. For an excellent discussion of the account and its implications, see Henry James and Greg Walker, "The Politics of *Gorboduc*," *English Historical Review* 110, no. 435 (February 1995): 109–21.

11. The other notable change is, of course, the title, which seems to be a strategy to get around Griffith's rights to the text, which had been duly licensed—Day's edition was unlicensed. For a full discussion, see Stephen Orgel, "The Book of the Play," in *From Performance to Print in Shakespeare's England*, ed. Peter Holland and Stephen Orgel (Houndmills: Palgrave Macmillan, 2006), 17–21.

12. The translation was first published in 1592 as *Antonius*, included in a volume with her translation of Philippe de Mornay's *Excellent discours de la vie et de la mort*, and reissued in 1595 under the title *The tragedie of Antonie* (London: William Ponsonby, 1595).

13. The play that in the court records is described as "huf, suff and ruf" is presumably *Cambises*.

14. Newton's translation of *Octavia* into pentameter couplets first appeared in 1569.

15. Ivan Lupić, *Subjects of Advice: Drama and Counsel from More to Shakespeare* (Philadelphia: University of Pennsylvania Press, 2019), 88–112. William A. Armstrong, "The Authorship and Political Meaning of *Cambises*," *English Studies* 31, no. 4 (1955): 289–99, makes a persuasive argument for the ethical seriousness of *Cambises*.

16. The letter has disappeared, but its recipient Arend van Buchel copied it and the accompanying drawing of the theater into his commonplace book, which has survived, and is in the library of the University of Utrecht. The entire letter is reprinted (in Latin, without a translation), by E. K. Chambers, *The Elizabethan Stage*, 4 vols. (Oxford: Clarendon Press, 1923), 2:361–62. A translation, with a reproduction of the drawing, is in Joseph Quincy Adams, *Shakespearean Playhouses* (Cambridge, MA: Riverside Press, 1917), 167, 169—the drawing is widely reproduced elsewhere.

17. It is possible that there was also a single performance at the Globe shortly after the court performance. For the arguments relating to Jonson's arrest, see Richard Dutton, *Mastering the Revels: The Regulation and Censorship of English Renaissance Drama* (Basingstoke: Macmillan, 1991), 12, 164; and Tom Cain, introduction to *Sejanus*, in *The Cambridge Edition of the Works of Ben Jonson*, ed. David Bevington, Martin Butler, and Ian Donaldson, 7 vols. (Cambridge: Cambridge University Press, 2012), 2:201. To summarize briefly, there is first the matter of the collaborator: Jonson claimed that for the stage play there was a coauthor, whose scenes he had removed in preparing the play for publication. The most likely collaborator would have been Chapman, but it has been cogently argued that the claim is a cover (there is no other contemporary reference to a collaborator), so that when Jonson was brought before the Privy Council on whatever the charges were, he could claim that the suspect sections were by the collaborator. The problem with all this is that if you work out the dates, the complaint can only have been about the play in print in the quarto of 1605—there was only the one performance, mentioned on the title page, in 1603, possibly followed by another at the Globe; these must have been before

Elizabeth's death, because thereafter the theaters were closed for over a year. The complaint, moreover, according to Jonson when he told Drummond about it in 1619, was brought by his "mortal enemy" the Earl of Northampton. Northampton had no position of power until after James's accession, and the quarto includes a commendatory poem by Chapman which praises Northampton; this cannot have been written before mid-1605, so Northampton cannot have brought the complaint yet. Therefore the problem is in the printed text, and is not anything the collaborator might have written. The best guess is that the point of the charge seems to be that the play is promoting rebellion against a withdrawn and autocratic monarch around the time of Ralegh's trial on sedition charges; and Jonson was a Catholic convert, and therefore automatically suspect as a dissident at this point.

18. There is no evidence about the reception of the equally classical *Poetaster*, performed at the Blackfriars in 1601, but the play was not popular enough to be revived—neither, for that matter, was *Sejanus*.

19. The plays for the most part do not survive. See Inga-Stina Ewbank, introduction to *Catiline*, in *Cambridge Edition of the Works of Ben Jonson*, 4:5–9.

20. Ewbank, introduction to *Catiline*, in *Cambridge Edition of the Works of Ben Jonson*, 4:6, citing G. E. Bentley, *Shakespeare and Jonson: Their Reputations in the Seventeenth Century Compared*, 2 vols. (Chicago: University of Chicago Press, 1945), 1:111. Bentley claimed that it was the most widely cited play of either Jonson or Shakespeare, but his methodology was immediately questioned, and will not stand up to scrutiny. That *Catiline* was Jonson's most widely cited play (which is not the same as calling it his most popular play) seems, however, beyond question. Its political relevance throughout the century is obvious.

21. Robert Herrick, "Upon M. Ben. Johnson. Epig.," *Hesperides or Noble Numbers* (London, (1648), 173. This is the only evidence that *The Alchemist* was ever hissed.

22. *Jonsonus Virbius* (1638), 27. The elegy here is anonymous, but subsequently appears as "An Epitaph on Ben. Johnson" in *J. Cleaveland Revived* (1659), 55–56.

23. *Jonsonus Virbius*, 17.

24. *Jonsonus Virbius*, 29.

25. *Jonsonus Virbius*, 53. The poem is by Ralph Brideoake, Cambridge scholar and later Bishop of Chichester.

26. By the Oxford scholar Richard West. *Jonsonus Virbius*, 57.

27. Ben Jonson, "To the memory of [. . .] Shakespeare," prefaced to the Shakespeare first folio, sig. *A4*$^{r-v}$.

CHAPTER 7

1. Stuart Gillespie, *English Translation and Classical Reception* (Chichester: Wiley-Blackwell, 2011), 151.

2. Margaret Cavendish, Duchess of Newcastle, *Poems and Fancies* (1653), 54–58. The passages cited are on p. 54.

3. George Chapman, *The Iliads of Homer Prince of Poets* (1611), sig. *A3*^{r}.

4. Thomas Grantham, *The First Booke of Homer's Iliads* (1659), sig. A2^{r}.

5. The Horace passage is *Ars Poetica*, line 359; in Ben Jonson's translation, "Sometimes I hear good Homer snore" (*Horace: Of the Art of Poetry*, line 536). The Dryden is from his preface to *The State of Innocence* (1677), sig. b1^{v}.

6. Alexander Pope, *An Essay on Criticism* (London, 1711), lines 178–79.

7. Matthew Arnold, *On Translating Homer: With F. W. Newman's "Homeric Translation" and Arnold's "Last Words,"* ed. W. H. D. Rouse (London: Routledge, [1905]), 37–38. To the best of my knowledge Arnold does not discuss the passage elsewhere.

8. Francis Bacon, *The Twoo Bookes* [. . .] *Of the proficience and advancement of Learning, divine and humane* (1605), fol. 23^{v}.

9. Thomas Browne, *Pseudodoxia Epidemica: or Enquiries into Very many received Tenents, And commonly presumed Truths* (1672), 21. My citations are from the last revised edition published during Browne's lifetime, which includes passages not in the first edition of 1646. For a fuller discussion, see my essay on the history of the concept of plagiarism, in which this account of Browne is included. Stephen Orgel, "Plagiarism and Original Sin," in *Plagiarism in Early Modern England*, ed. Paulina Kewes (Houndmills: Palgrave Macmillan, 2003), 56–73.

10. This and the following citations from Browne, *Pseudodoxia Epidemica*, are all on page 22.

11. Harold Ogden White, *Plagiarism and Imitation During the English Renaissance: A Study in Critical Distinctions* (Cambridge, MA: Harvard University Press, 1935), 75.

12. Information about Ogilby's early life derives mostly from John Aubrey's *Brief Lives.* See Charles W. J. Withers's article in the *DNB*, and Katherine S. van Eerde, *John Ogilby and the Taste of His Times* (Folkestone: William Dawson, 1976).

13. John Ogilby, trans., *The Works of Publius Virgilius Maro* (1649 and 1650), sig. A3^{r-v}.

14. John Ogilby, *The Entertainment of His Most Excellent Majestie Charles II in his Passage through the City of London to his Coronation* [. . .] (1662).

15. Thomas Hobbes, "To the Reader: Concerning the Vertues of an Heroique Poem," in *The Iliads and Odysses of Homer*, 2nd ed. (1677), sig. [1]A11^{v}.

16. John Dryden, *MacFlecknoe* (1692), lines 100–102; Alexander Pope, *The Dunciad* [. . .] *Variorum* (1729), 1.248.

17. Anthony Blackwall, *An Introduction to the Classics* (1728), 3.

18. Blackwall, *Introduction to the Classics*, 75.

19. Samuel Johnson, "Life of Pope," in *The Works of Samuel Johnson*, a new edition, in twelve volumes, with an essay on his life and genius by Arthur Murphy (1792), 11:83.

20. See, e.g., Norman Callan, "Pope's Iliad: A New Document," *Review of English Studies* 4, no. 14 (April 1953): 109–21, an analysis of proof sheets of the edition in which Pope is seen correcting the Greek quotations in the notes.

21. Johnson, "Life of Pope," 79.

22. Lionel Trilling, *Matthew Arnold*, rev. ed. (London: George Allen and Unwin, 1949), 169–70.

23. Trilling, *Matthew Arnold*, 168.

24. Trilling, *Matthew Arnold*, 172–73.

25. Arnold, *On Translating Homer*, ed. Rouse, 96.

26. Arnold, *On Translating Homer*, ed. Rouse, 104.

27. Alfred Tennyson, in *Enoch Arden and Other Poems* (1864), 167.

28. For example, it is clear that Arnold misunderstands the Greek hexameter, and makes the same mistake Campion makes, confusing stress with quantity.

29. W. H. D. Rouse, "Introductory," in Arnold, *On Translating Homer*, 1.

30. Newman, in *On Translating Homer*, ed. Rouse, 117.

31. Arnold, in *On Translating Homer*, ed. Rouse, 145.

32. Rouse, "Introductory," in Arnold, *On Translating Homer*, ed. Rouse, 20.

33. *Saturday Review*, April 25, 1863, 539–40.

34. Daniel Mendelsohn, review of Stanley Lombardo's translation of *The Iliad*, *New York Times Book Review*, July 20, 1997, 24.

35. Mendelsohn, *New York Times Book Review*, July 20, 1997, 24.

CODA

1. Mary Beard, "Are Classics Classy? The Roman View," *New York Review of Books*, accessed 6/23/2018, www.nybooks.com/daily/2009/12/16/are-classics-classy-the-roman-view/. For a more detailed account, see James Tatum, "What Was a Classic?", *Classical World* 114.1 (2020), pp. 85–97. I regret that this superb essay appeared too late for me to take it into account.

2. T. S. Eliot, "What Is a Classic?," in *On Poetry and Poets* (London: Faber and Faber, 1957), 54. The lecture was delivered in 1944, and first published in 1945.

3. Eliot, "What Is a Classic?," 55.

4. Eliot, "What Is a Classic?," 70.

5. Eliot, "What Is a Classic?," 61–62.

6. Eliot, "What Is a Classic?," 70.

7. Eliot, "What Is a Classic?," 69.

8. Italo Calvino, *Why Read the Classics?*, trans. Martin McLaughlin (New York: Pantheon Books, 1999), 3.

9. Calvino, *Why Read the Classics?*, 7.

10. Calvino, "The Odysseys Within *The Odyssey*," in *Why Read the Classics?*, 11.

Bibliography

PRIMARY SOURCES

Ascham, Roger. *The Scholemaster.* 1571.

Aubrey, John. *Aubrey's Brief Lives.* Edited by O. L. Dick. Ann Arbor, MI: University of Michigan Press, 1957.

Bacon, Francis. *The Twoo Bookes* [. . .] *Of the proficience and advancement of Learning, divine and humane.* London, 1605.

Beard, Thomas. *The Theatre of Gods Judgements.* 1597.

Birch, Thomas, comp. *The Court and Times of Charles the First: Containing a series of historical and confidential letters* [. . .]. 2 vols. London, 1848.

Blackwall, Anthony. *An Introduction to the Classics.* London, 1728.

Brende, John, trans. *The Actes of the Greate Alexander.* London: Richard Tottel, 1553.

Browne, Sir Thomas. *Pseudodoxia Epidemica: or Enquiries into Very many received Tenents, And commonly presumed Truths.* London, 1672.

Campion, Thomas. *Campion's Works.* Edited by Percival Vivian. Oxford: Oxford University Press, 1909.

———. *Observations in the Art of English Poesie.* 1602. In *Elizabethan Critical Essays*, edited by G. Gregory Smith, 2:327–55. 2 vols. Oxford: Oxford University Press, 1904.

Cartari, Vincenzo. *Le imagini de i dei de gli antichi.* Venice, 1587.

Cavendish, Margaret. *See* Newcastle, Duchess of.

Chapman, George. *The Divine Poem of Mvsaevs.* London, 1616.

———. *Homers Odysses.* London, 1616.

———. *The Iliads of Homer Prince of Poets.* London, 1611.

Comes, Natalis [or Natale Conti]. *Mythologiae.* Padua, 1616.

Daniel, Samuel. *A Defence of Ryme.* 1603. In *Elizabethan Critical Essays*, edited by G. Gregory Smith, 2:356–84. 2 vols. Oxford: Oxford University Press, 1904.

Deschamps, Eustache, *Œuvres complètes*, ed. A. H. E. de Queux de Saint-Hilaire and G. Raynaud, 11 vols. Paris: Firmin-Didot, 1878–1903.

Dolce, Lodovico. *Giocasta.* Venice, 1549.

———. *Le Tragedie.* Venice, 1566.

Douglas, Gavin, trans. *The xiii Bukes of Eneados* [. . .]. London, 1553.

Drant, Thomas. *Horace His Arte of Poetrie* [. . .]. London, 1567.

Dryden, John. *The State of Innocence.* London, 1677.

———. *The Works of Virgil.* London, 1697.

Erasmus, Desiderius. *De Ratione Studii.* Translated by W. H. Woodward. Cambridge: Cambridge University Press, 1904.

Fleming, Abraham, trans. *The Bucolics of Publius Virgilius Maro* [. . .] *Together with his Georgiks.* London, 1589.

Gager, William. *William Gager: The Complete Works.* Edited with translation and commentary by Dana Sutton. 4 vols. London: Routledge, 2019.

Gascoigne, George. *The Glasse of Government, etc.* Edited by John W. Cunliffe. Cambridge: Cambridge University Press, 1910.

———. *The Posies.* Edited by John W. Cunliffe. Cambridge: Cambridge University Press, 1907.

Giraldi, Lilio Gregorio. *De Deis Gentium.* Lyons, 1565.

Golding, Arthur. *The eyght bookes of Caius Iulius Cæsar* [. . .]. London, 1565.

———. *The Fyrst Fovver Bookes of P. Ouidius Nasos worke intitled Metamorphosis* [. . .]. London, 1565.

———. *The XV. bookes of P. Ouidius Naso, entituled, Metamorphosis.* London, 1567.

Grantham, Thomas. *The First Booke of Homer's Iliads.* London, 1659.

Greene, Robert. *Menaphon: Camillas alarum to slumbering Euphues.* London, 1589.

Hall, John. *Virgidemiarum.* London, 1599.

Harvey, Gabriel, to Edmund Spenser. "A Gallant Familiar Letter [. . .] (from Three Proper and Wittie Familiar Letters [. . .], 1580)." In *Elizabethan Critical Essays*, edited by G. Gregory Smith, 1:101–26. 2 vols. Oxford, 1904.

Haydocke, Richard. *A Tracte containing the Artes of curious Painting, Caruinge & Buildinge.* [translation of Paolo Lomazzo. *Trattato dell'arte della pittura scultura ed architettura.* Milan, 1584]. Oxford, 1598.

Herrick, Robert. *Hesperides or Noble Numbers.* London, 1648.

Hobbes, Thomas. *The Iliads and Odysses of Homer.* 2nd ed. 1677.

Holland, Philemon, trans. *The Historie of the World: Commonly called The Naturall Historie of C. Plinius Secundus.* London, 1601.

[Howard, Edward]. *Spencer Redivivus* [. . .] *By a Person of Quality.* London, 1687.

Howard, Henry. *See* Surrey, Earl of.

Johnson, Samuel. *The Works of Samuel Johnson.* A new edition, in twelve volumes. With an essay on his life and genius by Arthur Murphy. London, 1792.

Jonson, Ben. *The Cambridge Edition of the Works of Ben Jonson.* Edited by David Bevington, Martin Butler, and Ian Donaldson. 7 vols. Cambridge: Cambridge University Press, 2012.

Jonsonus Virbius. London, 1638.

Lomazzo, Paolo. *Trattato.* See Haydocke.

Marlowe, Christopher. *Certaine of Ovids Elegies.* Middleburgh, 1599.

——— *Christopher Marlowe: The Complete Poems and Translations.* Edited by Stephen Orgel. New York: Penguin Books, 2007.

Marlowe, Christopher, and George Chapman. *Hero and Leander.* London, 1598.

Medwall, Henry. *Fulgens and Lucres.* In *The Plays of Henry Medwall*, edited by Alan H. Nelson, 31–89. Cambridge: D. S. Brewer, 1980.

Meres, Francis. *Palladis Tamia: Wits Treasury; Being the Second Part of Wits Commonwealth.* London, 1598.

Montaigne, Michel de. *Essayes.* Translated by John Florio. London, 1613.

More, Thomas. *The Complete Works of St. Thomas More.* Vol. 8, *The Confutation of Tyndale's Answer.* Edited by Louis A. Schuster. New Haven: Yale University Press, 1973.

———. *The Latin Epigrams*. Edited by Leicester Bradner and Charles Arthur Lynch. Chicago: University of Chicago Press, 1953.

Nashe, Thomas. *The apologie of Pierce Pennilesse*. London, 1593.

Newcastle, Duchess of (Margaret Cavendish). *Poems and Fancies*. London, 1653.

Newman, Francis. See Arnold.

Newton, Thomas. *Seneca his tenne tragedies, translated into Englysh*. London, 1581.

Ogilby, John. *The Entertainment of His Most Excellent Majestie Charles II in his Passage through the City of London to his Coronation* [. . .]. London, 1662.

———. *Homer his Iliads Translated*. London, 1660.

———. *Homer his Odysses Translated*. London, 1665.

———, trans. *The Works of Publius Virgilius Maro*. London, 1649 and 1650.

Peacham, Henry. *The Compleat Gentleman*. London, 1634.

Phaer, Thomas. *The seuen first bookes of the Eneidos* [. . .]. London, 1558.

Pope, Alexander. *The Dunciad* [. . .] *Variorum*. London, 1729.

Preston, Thomas. *Cambises King of Percia*. London, 1569.

Prideaux, Humphrey. *Marmora Oxoniensia, ex Arundellianis* [. . .]. Oxford, 1676.

Rubens, Sir Peter Paul. *The Letters of Peter Paul Rubens*. Edited by R. S. Magurn. Cambridge, MA: Harvard University Press, 1955.

Sackville, Thomas, and Thomas Norton. *The Tragedie of Ferrex and Porrex*. London, 1570.

———. *The Tragedie of Gorboduc*. London, 1565.

Sandys, George. *Ovids Metamorphosis Englished*. London, 1626 and 1632.

Scaliger, Julius Caesar. *Poetices Libri Septem*. Lyons: Antoine Vincent, 1561.

Sidney, Mary, Countess of Pembroke. *The tragedie of Antonie*. London, 1595.

Sidney, Sir Philip. *An Apologie for Poetrie*. London, 1595.

———. *The Poems of Sir Philip Sidney*, ed. William A. Ringler. Oxford: Clarendon Press, 1962.

Smith, G. Gregory, ed. *Elizabethan Critical Essays*. 2 vols. Oxford: Oxford University Press, 1904 (and many later reprintings).

Spenser, Edmund. *The Faerie Queene*. London, 1590.

———. *The Faerie Queene* [etc.]. London, 1611–1613.

———. *The Second Part of The Faerie Queene*. London, 1596.

Stanyhurst, Richard, trans. *Thee First Foure Bookes of Virgil His Aeneis* [. . .]. Leiden, 1582.

Surrey, Earl of (Henry Howard). *Certain bokes of Virgiles Aeneis turned into English meter*. London, 1557.

———. *The Fourth Boke of Virgill* [. . .]. London, 1554.

———. *Songes and Sonnettes* [Tottel's Miscellany]. London, 1557.

Theocritus. *Sixe Idillia*. London, 1588.

Tottel, Richard, comp. *Songes and Sonettes Written By the Ryght Honorable Lord Henry Howard, late Earle of Surrey, and other* [Tottel's Miscellany]. London, 1557.

Udall, Nicholas. *Floures for Latine spekynge selected and gathered oute of Terence* [. . .]. London, 1534.

Webbe, William. *A Discourse of English Poetry* (1586). Edited by Sonia Hernández-Santano. Cambridge: Modern Humanities Research Association, 2016.

SECONDARY SOURCES

Armstrong, William A. "The Authorship and Political Meaning of *Cambises*." *English Studies* 31, no. 4 (1955): 289–99.

Arnold, Matthew. *On Translating Homer: With F. W. Newman's "Homeric Translation" and Arnold's "Last Words."* Edited by W. H. D. Rouse. London: Routledge, [1905].

Attridge, Derek. *Well-Weighed Syllables: Elizabethan Verse in Classical Metres.* Cambridge: Cambridge University Press, 1974.

Barkan, Leonard. *The Gods Made Flesh.* New Haven: Yale University Press, 1986.

Baron, Sabrina Alcorn. "Red Ink and Black Letter: Reading Early Modern Authority." In *The Reader Revealed*, edited by Sabrina Alcorn Baron, 19–30. Washington, DC: Folger Shakespeare Library, 2001.

Bate, Jonathan. *Shakespeare and Ovid.* Oxford: Oxford University Press, 1993.

———, ed. *Titus Andronicus.* The Arden Shakespeare. London: Routledge, 1995.

Beard, Mary. *Confronting the Classics.* New York: Liveright, 2013.

Bentley, G. E. *Shakespeare and Jonson: Their Reputations in the Seventeenth Century Compared.* 2 vols. Chicago: University of Chicago Press, 1945.

Berger, Susanna. "Meaning and Understanding in Intellectual History." *Global Intellectual History* 5, no. 3 (May 2020): 329–54. https://doi.org/10.1080/23801883.2020.1729463.

Binns, J. W. *Intellectual Culture in Elizabethan and Jacobean England.* Leeds: Francis Cairns, 1990.

Bland, Mark. "The Appearance of the Text in Early Modern England." *Text* 11 (1998): 91–154.

Braden, Gordon. *The Classics and English Renaissance Poetry: Three Case Studies.* New Haven: Yale University Press, 1978.

Braden, Gordon, Robert Cummings, and Stuart Gillespie, eds. *The Oxford History of Literary Translation in English.* Vol. 2, *1550–1660.* Oxford: Oxford University Press, 2010.

Bradner, Leicester. "The Authorship of *Spenser Redivivus.*" *Review of English Studies* 14 (1938): 323–26.

Brammall, Sheldon. *The English "Aeneid."* Edinburgh: Edinburgh University Press, 2015.

Braunmuller, A. R. "Accounting for Absence: The Transcription of Space." In *New Ways of Looking at Old Texts: Papers of the Renaissance English Text Society, 1985–1991*, edited by W. Speed Hill, 47–56. Binghamton, NY: Medieval and Renaissance Texts and Studies, 1993.

Cain, Tom. Introduction to *Sejanus.* In *The Cambridge Edition of the Works of Ben Jonson*, edited by David Bevington, Martin Butler, and Ian Donaldson, 2:197–209. 7 vols. Cambridge: Cambridge University Press, 2012.

Calasso, Roberto. *Le nozze di Cadmo e Armonia.* Milan: Adelphi, 1988. Translated by Tim Parks as *The Marriage of Cadmus and Harmony* (New York: Alfred A. Knopf, 1993).

Callan, Norman. "Pope's Iliad: A New Document." *Review of English Studies* 4, no. 14 (April 1953): 109–21.

Calvino, Italo. *Why Read the Classics?* Translated by Martin McLaughlin. New York: Pantheon, 1999.

Carlson, David. "Woodcut Illustrations of the Canterbury Tales, 1483–1602." *The Library*, 6th ser., 19 (1997): 25–67.

———. "The Writings of Bernard André." *Renaissance Studies* 12, no. 2 (June 1998): 229–50.

Cave, Terence. *The Cornucopian Text.* Oxford: Oxford University Press, 1979.

Chambers, E. K. *The Elizabethan Stage.* 4 vols. Oxford: Clarendon Press, 1923.

Cheney, Patrick. *Marlowe's Counterfeit Profession.* Toronto: University of Toronto Press, 1997.

Copeland, Rita, ed. *The Oxford History of Classical Reception in English Literature.* Vol. 1, *800–1558.* Oxford: Oxford University Press, 2016.

Cummings, Robert. "Translation and Literary Innovation." In *The Oxford History of Literary Translation in English.* Vol. 2, *1550–1660*, edited by Gordon Braden, Robert Cummings, and Stuart Gillespie, 32–44. Oxford: Oxford University Press, 2010.

Dennys, Rodney. *Heraldry and the Heralds*. London: Jonathan Cape, 1982.

Driver, Martha. "Ideas of Order: Wynkyn de Worde and the Title Page." In *Texts and Their Contexts: Papers from the Early Book Society*, edited by John Scattergood and Julia Boffey, 87–149. Dublin: Four Courts Press, 1997.

———. "Woodcuts and Decorative Techniques." In *A Companion to the Early Printed Book in Britain, 1476–1558*, edited by Vincent Gillespie and Susan Powell, 95–123. Cambridge: D. S. Brewer, 2014.

Dutton, Richard. *Mastering the Revels: The Regulation and Censorship of English Renaissance Drama*. Basingstoke: Macmillan, 1991.

Eerde, Katherine S. van. *John Ogilby and the Taste of His Times*. Folkestone: William Dawson, 1976.

Eliot, T. S. "What Is a Classic?" In *On Poetry and Poets*, 52–74. London: Faber and Faber, 1957.

Ellis, Roger, ed. *The Oxford History of Literary Translation in English*. Vol. 1, *To 1550*. Oxford: Oxford University Press, 2008.

Ewbank, Inga-Stina. Introduction to *Catiline*. In *The Cambridge Edition of the Works of Ben Jonson*, edited by David Bevington, Martin Butler, and Ian Donaldson, 4:3–21. 7 vols. Cambridge: Cambridge University Press, 2012.

Fernández, José María Pérez, and Edward Wilson-Lee, eds. *Translation and the Book Trade in Early Modern Europe*. Cambridge: Cambridge University Press, 2014.

Frampton, Stephanie Ann. *Empire of Letters*. New York: Oxford University Press, 2019.

Galbraith, Steven. "Edmund Spenser and the History of the Book, 1569–1679." PhD diss., Ohio State University, 2006.

Gillespie, Stuart. *English Translation and Classical Reception*. Chichester: Wiley-Blackwell, 2011.

———. "Statius in English, 1648–1747." *Translation and Literature* 8, no. 2 (1999): 157–75.

Gillespie, Vincent, and Susan Powell, eds. *A Companion to the Early Printed Book in Britain, 1476–1558*. Cambridge: D. S. Brewer, 2014.

Goldberg, Jonathan. "Sodomy and Society: The Case of Christopher Marlowe." In *Staging the Renaissance*, edited by David Scott Kastan and Peter Stallybrass, 75–82. New York: Routledge, 1991.

Golding, L. T. *An Elizabethan Puritan: Arthur Golding*. New York: Richard R. Smith, 1937.

Grafton, Anthony. *Commerce with the Classics*. Ann Arbor: University of Michigan Press, 1997.

Halperin, David. *One Hundred Years of Homosexuality*. New York: Routledge, 1990.

Herford, C. H., Percy Simpson, and Evelyn Simpson, eds. *Ben Jonson*. Vol. 10, *Play Commentary, Masque Commentary*. Oxford: Clarendon Press, 1950.

Honan, Park. *Christopher Marlowe, Poet and Spy*. Oxford: Oxford University Press, 2005.

Howarth, David. *Lord Arundel and His Circle*. New Haven: Yale University Press, 1985.

James, Henry, and Greg Walker. "The Politics of *Gorboduc*." *English Historical Review* 110, no. 435 (February 1995): 109–21.

James, Susan. "Edward Seymour, Duke of Somerset? Re-Examining a Tudor Portrait." *British Art Journal* 2, no. 2 (2000): 14–21.

Kerrigan, William, and Gordon Braden. *The Idea of the Renaissance*. Baltimore: Johns Hopkins University Press, 1989.

Kiséry, András. "An Author and a Bookshop: Publishing Marlowe's Remains at the Black Bear." *Philological Quarterly* 91, no. 3 (Summer 2012): 361–92.

Lesser, Zachary. "Typographic Nostalgia: Play-Reading, Popularity, and the Meanings of Black Letter." In *The Book of the Play*, edited by Marta Straznicky, 99–127. Amherst: University of Massachusetts Press, 2006.

Lupić, Ivan. "The Mobile Queen: Observing Hecuba in Renaissance Europe." *Renaissance Drama* 46, no. 1 (2018): 25–56.

———. *Subjects of Advice: Drama and Counsel from More to Shakespeare.* Philadelphia: University of Pennsylvania Press, 2019.

MacCulloch, Diarmaid. *Tudor Church Militant.* London: Penguin Books, 1999.

Marotti, Arthur. *Manuscript, Print, and the English Renaissance Lyric.* Ithaca: Cornell University Press, 1995.

Mathiessen, F. O. *Translation: An Elizabethan Art.* Cambridge, MA: Harvard University Press, 1931.

Mayor, A. Hyatt. *Prints and People: A Social History of Printed Pictures.* New York: Metropolitan Museum of Art, 1971.

McDonald, Russ. "Jonsonian Comedy and the Value of *Sejanus*." *Studies in English Literature* 21, no. 2 (1981): 287–305.

McLaughlin, Martin, Ingrid D. Rowland, and Elisabetta Tarantino, eds. *Authority, Innovation and Early Modern Epistemology.* Leeds: Legenda, 2015.

Medcalf, Stephen. "Classical Authors." In *The Oxford History of Literary Translation in English.* Vol. 1, *To 1550*, edited by Roger Ellis, 364–89. Oxford: Oxford University Press, 2008.

Mendelson, E. Review of *Waiting for the Barbarians: Essays from the Classics to Pop Culture*, by Daniel Mendelsohn. *New York Review of Books* 59, no. 16 (2012): 26–29.

Millar, Oliver. *The Queen's Pictures.* New York: Macmillan, 1977.

Milne, Kirsty. "The Forgotten Greek Books of Elizabethan England." *Literature Compass* 4, no. 3 (2007): 677–87.

Moroney, Davitt. "Thomas Morley Portrayed." (forthcoming).

Nicholl, Charles. *The Reckoning: The Murder of Christopher Marlowe.* London: Cape, 1992.

Norbrook, David. *Writing the English Republic: Poetry, Rhetoric and Politics, 1627–1660.* Cambridge: Cambridge University Press, 1999.

Orgel, Stephen. "The Book of the Play." In *From Performance to Print in Shakespeare's England*, edited by Peter Holland and Stephen Orgel, 13–54. Houndmills: Palgrave Macmillan, 2006.

———. "Measuring Verse, Measuring Value in English Renaissance Poetry." In *Authority, Innovation and Early Modern Epistemology*, edited by Martin McLaughlin, Ingrid D. Rowland, and Elisabetta Tarantino, 97–103. Leeds: Legenda, 2015.

———. "Plagiarism and Original Sin." In *Plagiarism in Early Modern England*, edited by Paulina Kewes, 56–73. Houndmills: Palgrave Macmillan, 2003.

———. *The Reader in the Book.* Oxford: Oxford University Press, 2015.

———. "Textual Icons: Reading Early Modern Illustrations." In *Spectacular Performances*, 180–87. Manchester: Manchester University Press, 2011.

Papadopoulou, Thalia. *Euripides: Phoenician Women.* London: Duckworth, 2008.

Pearcy, L. T. *The Mediated Muse: English Translations of Ovid 1560–1600.* Hamden, CT: Archon Books, 1984.

Prosperi, Valentina. "The Place of the Father: The Reception of Homer in the Renaissance Canon." In *Brill's New Pauly Supplements Online* 1. Vol. 5, *The Reception of Classical Literature.* (accessible on the Internet through participating institutions)

Rhodes, Neil, and Jonathan Sawday. *The Renaissance Computer.* London: Routledge, 2000.

Riggs, David. *The World of Christopher Marlowe.* New York: Henry Holt, 2004.

Rouse, W. H. D. *See* Arnold.

Simpson, James. "The *Aeneid* Translations of Henry Howard, Earl of Surrey." In *The Oxford History of Classical Reception in English Literature.* Vol. 1, *800–1558*, edited by Rita Copeland, chap. 28. Oxford: Oxford University Press, 2015.

Starnes, D. T., and E. W. Talbert. *Classical Myth and Legend in Renaissance Dictionaries*. Chapel Hill: University of North Carolina Press, 1955.

Strong, Roy. *Henry Prince of Wales and England's Lost Renaissance*. London: Thames and Hudson, 1986.

———. *Tudor and Jacobean Portraits*. London: H.M. Stationery Office, 1969.

Sweeney, John G., III. "Sejanus and the People's Beastly Rage." *ELH* 48, no. 1 (Spring 1981): 61–82.

Talbert, E. W. "Current Scholarly Works and the Erudition of Jonson's *Masque of Augurs*." *Studies in Philology* 44 (1947): 605–24.

Trilling, Lionel. *Matthew Arnold*. Rev. ed. London: George Allen and Unwin, 1949.

Wakelin, Daniel. *Humanism, Reading, and English Literature, 1430–1530*. Oxford: Oxford University Press, 2007.

———. "Humanism and Printing." In *A Companion to the Early Printed Book in Britain, 1476–1558*, edited by Vincent Gillespie and Susan Powell, 227–47. Cambridge: D. S. Brewer, 2014.

Walker, Greg. *The Politics of Performance in Early Renaissance Drama*. Cambridge: Cambridge University Press, 1998.

Wallace, Andrew. *Virgil's Schoolboys*. Oxford: Oxford University Press, 2010.

White, Harold Ogden. *Plagiarism and Imitation During the English Renaissance: A Study in Critical Distinctions*. Cambridge, MA: Harvard University Press, 1935.

Willoughby, James. "Universities, Colleges and Chantries." In *A Companion to the Early Printed Book in Britain, 1476–1558*, edited by Vincent Gillespie and Susan Powell, 207–24. Cambridge: D. S. Brewer, 2014.

Wright, A. D. *In Search of Christopher Marlowe*. New York: Vanguard Press, 1965.

Wright, Clare. "Henry Medwall, *Fulgens and Lucres*." In *The Oxford Handbook of Tudor Drama*, edited by Thomas Betteridge and Greg Walker, 177–91. Oxford: Oxford University Press, 2012.

Index